The Connecting CHURCH 2.0

Also by Randy Frazee

The Connecting Church

The Christian Life Profile Assessment Tool Workbook

The Heart of the Story

Making Room for Life

Real Simplicity

(expanded edition of *Making Room for Life*; with Rozanne Frazee)

Renovation of the Heart: An Interactive Student Edition

(with Dallas Willard)

The Connecting CHURCH 2.0

BEYOND SMALL GROUPS
TO AUTHENTIC COMMUNITY

2.0

RANDY FRAZEE

FOREWORD BY MAX LUCADO

ZONDERVAN®

ZONDERVAN.com/
AUTHORTRACKER
follow your favorite authors

We want to hear from you. Please send your comments about this book to us in care of zreview@zondervan.com. Thank you.

ZONDERVAN

The Connecting Church 2.0
Copyright © 2013 by Randy Frazee

This title is also available as a Zondervan ebook. Visit www.zondervan.com/ebooks.

Requests for information should be addressed to:

Zondervan, Grand Rapids, Michigan 49530

Library of Congress Cataloging-in-Publication Data

Frazee, Randy.
    The connecting church 2.0 : beyond small groups to authentic community / Randy Frazee.
        p. cm.
    Includes bibliographical references.
    ISBN 978-0-310-49435-5 (pbk.)
      1. Communities—Religious aspects—Christianity. 2. Communities—Biblical teaching. 3. Church. 4. Community life—United States. 5. Small groups—Religious aspects. I. Title.
BV4517.5.F73 2013
250—dc23
                                               2012036670

Cover design: Tobias' Outerware for Books
Interior design: David Conn

Printed in the United States of America

15 16 17 18 19 20 /QG/ 20 19 18 17 16 15 14 13 12 11 10 9 8 7 6 5 4 3 2 1

In memory of my mother,
Ruth Ann Frazee

CONTENTS

CONTENTS

FOREWORD BY MAX LUCADO

What was the mightiest miracle of the first New Testament church? As you mentally thumb through the book of Acts, think of the greatest event. Many good answers surface:

- the falling of the Holy Spirit in the upper room
- the baptism of three thousand souls on the day of Pentecost
- the healing of the crippled man at the temple gate
- the conversion of Saul or the release of Peter or the vision of Stephen

Mighty miracles, for sure. If you would list any of them as the greatest of the New Testament church, I wouldn't blame you. But then again, I wouldn't agree with you. As great as these are, I feel there is one even greater. One that is often overlooked, easily neglected, but absolutely amazing. What is this mighty miracle? Unity. This church loved each other.

> All the believers were together and shared everything. They would sell their land and the things they owned and then divide the money and give it to anyone who needed it. The believers met together in the Temple every day. They ate together in their homes, happy to share their food with joyful hearts. They praised God and were liked by all the people. Every day the Lord added those who were being saved to the group of believers.
>
> Acts 2:44–46 NCV

This was a dynamic church: "Every day the Lord added those who were being saved to the group of believers." Membership went from zero to three thousand overnight! Every meeting had more faces; every service had new members. The Jerusalem 101 class was bursting at the seams!

This was a diverse church. "We are from different places: Parthia, Media, Elam, Mesopotamia, Judea, Cappadocia, Pontus, Asia, Phrygia, Pamphylia, Egypt, the areas of Libya near Cyrene, Rome (both Jews and those who had become Jews), Crete, and Arabia" (Acts 2:8–11 NCV). Fifteen different regions were represented! Jews came from all over the world. Some, like the Parthinians, were from the east. Others, like the Egyptians, were from the south. And some, like the Romans, from the north. Their food was different; their cultures different; their heart languages different. They came to be a part of the Passover; they stayed to be a part of the church.

Within a short time, according to Acts 4:4, the church grew to five thousand male members, which means as many as twenty thousand men, women, and children were a part of this fellowship. Many of them were from other lands. They had no place to sleep or eat. So what happened? How did they survive? "All the believers were together and shared everything. They would sell their land and the things they owned and then divide the money and give it to anyone who needed it."

How can fellowship be born of such diversity? How can you feel a part of a church that seems to change every day? How can you feel at home when you are meeting new people at every service? Many church members ask the same questions today. Succinctly stated, it goes like this: How can we connect? With each other? With our neighbors? In our communities?

My friend Randy Frazee has spent a lifetime studying this question. Part pastor, part sociologist, he has made connection his passion. He has much to teach us.

I am blessed to have a front-row seat. As his coworker in the Oak Hills Church of San Antonio, Texas, I am able to watch the wonder of a connecting church. Under his leadership the connective tissue of the congregation is growing stronger. More people are finding their place. Most of all, more people are finding Christ.

I commend Randy and his teachings to you without hesitation. There is something in these pages for every person, from sincere seeker to seasoned follower. Randy's enthusiasm is contagious. Unity happened in the first-century church. May it happen again!

PREFACE TO THE SECOND EDITION

It has been ten years since the first edition of *The Connecting Church* was released. Wow! A whole decade. When I turned ten, it had taken an entire lifetime to get there. Now I feel a little like Rip Van Winkle—like I took a nap and woke up to find a decade gone. And the speed of change has been even faster than the ticking of a clock. Without question, someone forgot to put a governor on change; it no longer adheres to the speed limit we thought we had.

Think of the changing rate of technological advances. The first computer came out in 1939. It was the size of a typical dining room—the whole room! It took thirty-five more years for the first personal computer to come out. It fit on a desktop. The first notebook computer came out ten years later.[1] It fit in a briefcase. Four years after that, all the programs and data that once fit into my notebook computer are in my smartphone, and I can retrieve them faster than ever. The phone fits into my pocket. As amazing as this is, I am confident that just in the time it takes these words to make it to the shelf of a bookstore (assuming printed books are still around a year from now), some better, smarter, and faster device will be available.

While technology has created all kinds of new revenue streams and new opportunities to stay connected to people around the world, its change rate has also accelerated our loneliness. More and more folks, young and old, rely almost exclusively on the technology of e-mail, texting, Twitter, and Facebook for their relationships—and they will also rely on the new things invented tomorrow. In addition, many people create an online avatar that is utterly different from the person they really are.

You don't have to take a class in sociology to know this won't cut it. You don't have to go to seminary to know this is no substitute for the way God designed for us to live. We were wired to require eye-to-eye contact. We were created for real hugs. While technology can be a good supplement and time-saver, it is not a replacement for a good ole-fashioned dinner with your family or holding the hand of a friend in trouble. Nothing can replace hanging out in the same room where someone involuntarily breaks out in an all-out belly laugh. Virtual condolences will never match the power of simply "being there" when a friend is bruised in a relationship or broken by an unexpected announcement.

Think of the cultural and economic changes in the United States since the new millennium began. The year 2001, when the first edition of *The Connecting Church* was published, introduced a permanent shift in this country. The attacks on September 11 changed the way we understood ourselves as a nation, perhaps forever. Since then we've been at war and experienced a crash in our housing market. While there is still an unbelievable sense of opportunity and optimism among many Americans, there is also a growing notion that maybe we are at an irreversible tipping point. Some even fear we may be entering a permanent downward economic spiral. Our sixteen trillion dollar debt and an out-of-control rise in government spending can make the economy seem like a proverbial house of cards.

In one sense, I hope things get better. And yet in another sense, maybe it is a good thing we are where we are. When I did my initial research in the late 1990s, social scientists were suggesting that the only possible situation that might disrupt the negative cycle of "individualism, isolation, consumerism" in America was an economic collapse. As long as Americans have so much discretionary money, they will continue to purchase products and engage in activities that will further fragment their lives and keep them from looking for real, God-ordained solutions that bring genuine happiness. In recent years, however, rising fuel prices have caused folks to think twice about getting on a plane or taking a road trip for a vacation, opting to stay home instead. Now many of us have a fresh opportunity to dig some deeper roots in our community and engage with our neighbors. While we may lose our financial strength and curb our mobility, we also may gain something that will genuinely increase our joy and longevity — connected relationships, community. Maybe this is an acceptable swap.

I am convinced more than ever that the journey on which God placed my family and those who ventured out with us years ago remains the optimal course for the future. A few years into this radical journey, we thought of ourselves as pioneers, cutting a fresh trail with a social machete and without much hope of actually reaching the new world ourselves. We thought God might have called us to play the role of Abraham, who ventured out on the journey of promise but never enjoyed the land of promise. We thought we might be to this movement what John Wycliffe and John Huss were to the Reformation. They carried the same values and vision as Martin Luther but were a little before their time and were consequently burned at the stake for their stance. Their lives and courage contributed to the movement, but they would never see the Reformation themselves. We had come to grips with playing this same role in church history in our small corner of the world. But now I am not so sure. With the rate of change in our culture and the nature of the shifts themselves, we just might see much of what we dreamed come to pass in our lifetime.

Following the release of *The Connecting Church* in 2001, I spent four more spectacular years (actually the best) at Pantego Bible Church in Fort Worth, where the journey began for us. Then, with the sense of God's call to expand our territory, I spent three years to the day as a teaching pastor at Willow Creek Community Church, where I was charged with implementing the principles of this book in the Chicagoland area. In 2008, we jumped on a one-way plane back to Texas, this time to San Antonio. I took over the role of senior minister from legendary pastor and author Max Lucado at Oak Hills Church. Max has remained on staff as a full-time teacher, partner, and, most of all, a really great friend. Truthfully, there have been times I felt alone in my quest, but God has assured me time and time again that there are others dreaming the same dream. As he did with Elijah, so God has reminded me that there are others who embrace the vision. I am not alone.

I am excited to update you on my journey—what I have learned, what has worked ... and what has not!

The first two chapters of parts 1 through 3 remain largely unaltered from the first edition. While I have added some new insights from research, writings, and experiences that have occurred within the last few years, the principles are timeless and, I believe, prophetic for our current time. The methods of applying these principles, however, remain fluid, constantly changing. And in the last ten years, I have sensed strongly that something new and yet ancient is emerging. Therefore, the last chapters of parts 1, 2, and 3 contain completely new material. These chapters represent the best thoughts and practices for applying the principles I know of to date. Still ... buyer, beware! The best practices for establishing and leading a healthy culture of community will continue to evolve, leaving the door open for *The Connecting Church 3.0* in another ten (if not two) years from now!

Part 4 is a brand-new offering devoted to the corporate implementation of the connecting church principles laid out in parts 1, 2, and 3. In chapter 12, I share honestly about the top ten mistakes I made in ministry, the lessons I learned, and the ways I've sought to correct those mistakes. Then, if you are serious about discovering authentic community through the church, I believe you will need to choose one of two paths laid out in chapter 13 and then addressed individually in chapters 14 and 16. The first path is the more conventional one and the focus of chapter 14. It involves a hybrid approach, mobilizing people who gather in a central church building to find their primary core community for belonging, growing, and serving in their neighborhood. A decade of trial and error has led to some exciting "tweaks" on what I presented in the first edition.

Over these last ten years, it has been rewarding to see the number of early adopter learners who have grabbed hold of the principles and implemented them in their own context, in their own way. With great courage and resolve, these friends stir in their souls, work out with their minds, and apply in their lives what God is revealing to them. Before we move on to the second path in chapter 16, chapter 15 exposes you to four churches of different sizes and in different places that are successfully implementing a connecting church vision. As I write this, our team at Oak Hills is traveling in less than a month to one of those churches to learn from them. I encourage you to do the same as you seek the right model for your context.

The last chapter, chapter 16, is devoted to the second and unconventional path introduced in chapter 13. What if a small band of believers who gathered in their neighborhood to belong, grow, and serve became a church? This would free up massive margin in time and money to devote to ministering in their neighborhood, city, and even the world. Technology has now given us the opportunity to deliver teaching and training through the Internet for a fraction of the cost of delivering teaching and training with buildings and large, paid staffs. I will lay out what I believe is the best idea for what this might look like for those God is stirring to try it.

As I wrote in the first edition, "My prayer is that the words in this book and the experience of our particular church will contribute positively to an outbreak of authentic community in the Christian church." This is still my prayer today.

Randy Frazee,
San Antonio, Texas,
March 2012

Chapter 1

THE LONELIEST NATION
ON EARTH

The Johnsons appear to have a wonderful life. They own a house in a nice suburb with four bedrooms, two baths, and a rear-entry, two-car garage. Their house is surrounded by a six-foot-high fence to provide privacy for an inground pool, a barbecue grill, and patio furniture. Bob and Karen have two children—a boy and a girl. Bob and Karen each have a college degree, and they both have jobs that provide a combined household income well above the average for their community. Most important, everyone in the family is in good health.

Yet, if you could enter the hearts and thoughts of Bob and Karen Johnson, you would discover that they have dreams and fears no one else knows about. While they have never voiced it to anyone, there is an increasing sense of isolation, distress, and powerlessness growing inside them. In a nutshell, the Johnsons have done a fine job of "keeping up with the Joneses," but they still are not happy.

How could this be? The Johnsons are living the American Dream. So many people are less fortunate. But their personal dilemma—the isolation and distress that quietly gnaws away at their contentment—is a national epidemic. And their experience is no surprise to sociologists and pollsters. George Gallup Jr. concluded from his studies and polls that Americans are among the loneliest people in the world.[1] This seems unbelievable when you think of the easy access to transportation and the billions of dollars of discretionary money available for entertainment. Americans can buy so much activity. How can they possibly be so lonely? We are surrounded by more people than ever before in the history of our country. With these undeniable benefits in place, how could a Gallup poll rank us among the loneliest people in the world?

Let's take a closer look at Bob and Karen's story. Eight years ago, Bob took a job at an office located in a growing suburb in another city. Although moving there took them farther from their families, both Bob and Karen had agreed it would still be feasible to fly home on occasion because Bob would be making more money and the airport was in close proximity to their new home.

Bob and Karen both rise at 6:30 a.m. On this day, Bob hurries to leave the house at 7:00 to beat the rush hour traffic; doing so allows him to get to work in thirty-five minutes as opposed to fifty-five minutes. He opens the door leading into the garage, hits the garage door opener, gets into his car, and pulls out of the driveway. He spots his new neighbor taking out the trash and waves to him with a forced smile on his face. As Bob drives down the street, he reminds himself that this neighbor has been in the neighborhood now for two years and he still can't remember his name. This thought lasts for about five seconds before Bob turns on some music and his mind turns to the matters of the day.

Karen has worked out an arrangement to be at work at 9:00 a.m. so she can drop off her two children at school at 8:15. There is the usual rush to get her and the two children ready on time and out the door by 7:55, and today she manages to pull it off. With the same ritual precision, Karen makes her way to the car and starts heading out of the driveway when her son announces he left a lunch behind. The easiest move for Karen would be to go back in through the front door, but she sees her next-door neighbor, one of the few retired people in the area, beginning her yard work for the day. While Karen would love to catch up with her elderly neighbor, she is afraid if they engage in a conversation the children will be late for school, and then she'll be late for work. So rather than risk being late, Karen makes her way back to the rear-entry garage, opens the door with the automatic opener, and goes inside. As she grabs the forgotten lunch from the kitchen table, she realizes she has forgotten to set the security system. Once this is accomplished, off she goes again.

Bob and Karen encounter an average day at work: nine-and-a-half hours at the office, completing only four-and-a-half hours of actual productive work, as seems to be common in the American office environment. Both will bring home bulging briefcases in the hopes of sneaking in another hour of work after the children are in bed. At 3:30, the children go to their after-school program and wait for Mom or Dad to pick them up.

It is 5:00 p.m., and Bob absolutely must leave the office if he is to pick up the children from the after-school program on time. But as often happens, Bob doesn't leave until 5:20, and he gets trapped in a ten-minute traffic jam because of a stalled car on the freeway. He arrives thirty minutes late. Everyone is just a little edgy.

Bob and the kids pull into the rear-entry garage at 6:15. Bob turns off the security system, which assures him that no one has tampered with their home while they've been gone. Karen arrives at 6:30. The first order of business is dinner. Bob and Karen agreed, with a little help from a family therapist, that with Karen working to help pay the bills (especially the mortgage), sharing household chores was going to be a vital part of suburban life; Bob would need to share the load with her in the evenings.

While the children watch television, Mom and Dad are working together to heat up a tray of frozen lasagna and garlic bread. After dinner, the dishes are cleaned up, the mail is perused, homework papers are checked, and the children get ready for bed. It is now 9:00 p.m. The children are a half hour late getting to bed, but it was the best they could do.

At 9:15, Bob and Karen finally sit down. They are too exhausted to talk, so the television gets beamed on, right in the middle of a prime-time drama. They both watch television until the news is over, look at their briefcases for a moment, and agree to let the work go undone. Finally, at 11:30, they crawl into bed. A couple of words are exchanged, mostly businesslike talk concerning tomorrow's details.

As they close their eyes, they both gratefully ponder how easy this day had been compared to what is ahead. The remainder of the weeknights ahead will be filled with sports practices and games, music lessons, and a couple of evening work meetings.

While that constitutes the pattern during the week, Saturday and Sunday are primarily used for three activities: house and lawn care, children's sports, and church. These activities take up most of the available hours. But on the average weekend a few hours of open time is available for soaking in life with family and friends.

The problem the Johnsons have is common for many couples. First, their extended family members live in other cities around the United States. Second, they were so busy during the week that they didn't make plans to spend time with another family. Finally, while they would be open to spending some *spontaneous* time with the neighbors, no one is out in their front yards except a few men mowing their lawns, with earbuds attached to an iPod tucked in their khaki-colored shorts. Everyone else is either away from home or safely sheltered inside their centrally air-conditioned/ heated homes, fully equipped with cable television or a satellite dish. Or if not inside the house, they're in their backyards, which are completely landscaped for privacy.

Occasionally, an outing is planned with another couple or family who may live in another part of town. The time always seems to be a positive experience. Yet, because few of the gatherings are routinely with the same family, neither Bob nor Karen feels comfortable sharing their deepest dreams and fears with any of those people. Another weekend comes to a close with unvoiced stress and boredom, and Bob and Karen individually conclude that this was just an unusual week; next week will be better. Well, eight years have now passed since they adopted their American Dream lifestyle, with somewhere around 416 weeks classified as "unusual."

Oh, there is one more important aspect to the Johnsons' life. Bob and Karen are Christians. They attend church just about every Sunday and have been involved in a church-sponsored small group for a little over a year. The group is made up of other couples of roughly the same age and meets in one of the members' homes every other week. The Sunday worship services are usually uplifting and inspiring. Bob and Karen feel a sense of satisfaction with their children's involvement in the Sunday school program. As a matter of fact, it was their desire to give their children a religious and spiritual foundation that brought them back to church after a lapse during college and their early years of marriage. While the church is extremely friendly, the only people they really know are those who attend their small group.

The Johnsons' small group usually meets on the first and third Thursday night of each month from 7:00 to 9:30. The members of the group rotate the task of hosting the meeting in their homes. Most of the members live about ten to twenty minutes away from each other.

Bob and Karen joined the group in the hopes of finding a surrogate extended family, or at least a set of close friends with whom they could share their dreams and fears. But after a year of faithful attendance at the group, the Johnsons started to miss some of the meetings. Why? For several reasons. First, with their tight weekday schedule, it was difficult to eat dinner, check homework papers, bathe the children, pick up a babysitter, drive to the small group get-together by 7:00, leave around 10:15, take the babysitter back home, and return home around 11:30. This routine simply exhausted this couple, who were in search of meaningful friendships and a sense of personal peace.

A second reason the small group diminished in priority was the children's sports games and practices. Both children play soccer and basketball, which means that at least one if not both of them have either a practice or a game on Thursday nights.

A third reason was disappointment over how seldom members of the group got together outside of the regularly scheduled meetings. Everyone seemed to have a mutual desire to get together, but something always seemed to prevent more relaxed and spontaneous outings. Because the group only saw each other for a few hours twice (sometimes only once) a month, there wasn't the sense of intimacy the Johnsons wanted in order to freely share their dreams and fears. While they would consider their small group members to be their closest friends, the Johnsons long for something more.

To look at the outside shell of the Johnsons' life, it would appear they have it all together, yet on the inside they are two of the statistically lonely people about whom George Gallup Jr. writes. Bob and Karen are just two of the millions of Americans who are searching to belong. Moreover, what is true of the Johnson family is intensified in the single-parent home. Activity for the single parent is often doubled, practically eliminating any time for the development of personal relationships. In addition, the single parent often has to burn a great deal of additional energy negotiating with the ex-spouse.

The single adult without children is not exempt from loneliness. While more time can be allocated to enhancing adult relationships instead of managing children's activities, the additional time available does not mean they are not at home many hours, feeling deeply alone. While they may have an active group of acquaintances, most singles still long for deeper companionship than what seems to be in their grasp. One of the most significant struggles for a single person living in suburban America is the lack of wholesome gathering spots for singles. The lack of access to community means that isolation rules.

The purpose of this book is to help people who feel like the Johnsons find what they are searching for, to help people discover a rich sense of community. To belong! In our journey of discovery, we will explore three obstacles that hinder our attainment of biblical community in America, and we will look at three comprehensive and practical solutions to overcome these obstacles. These three solutions will be broken down further and defined in the fifteen characteristics that must be present for true Christian community to be experienced. The promise of this book is that restructuring our lifestyles around these fifteen characteristics will fulfill our "search to belong" and give us the rich, enduring fellowship we were created by God to experience.

Chapter 2

CREATED FOR COMMUNITY

A number of years ago, my wife and I finally cracked under the pleas of our children to add a dog to the family, giving in after eleven years of begging. Two days before Christmas, we purchased a full-bred beagle puppy we named Lady. She had lived with us for about a year when we took a family vacation without her. The children were very concerned about Lady's well-being while we were away and insisted that if we couldn't take her with us, we had to get her the best possible accommodations. Through the help of another pet-obsessed friend, we located a place—The Pet Hotel.

Imagine that, a hotel for pets! This was the first I had ever heard of such a thing. Each pet was assigned an individual room. A television played during the day for the dog to watch. The feedings were at precisely the time we offered them in her normal routine. The pets were actually walked and doted on more at The Pet Hotel than at home. This made the children feel better and made me feel a little poorer. (I've never been able to tell my father that I spent hard-earned money for an animal to stay in a pet hotel. For anyone born during the Depression, this would be an incomprehensible decision.)

The family returned home on a Friday night, too late to pick up Lady. So the first order of business on Saturday was to head to The Pet Hotel. We gathered all her personal belongings, received a report assuring us that they had done everything they promised, and paid the bill. When we got into the car, each of us eagerly petted Lady, genuinely happy to have her back. As we petted her, however, large clumps of hair clung to our hands. While I tried to convince the children that everything was OK, I was thoroughly concerned.

When we arrived home, I called the veterinarian in a panic. When I explained our dog's symptoms upon picking her up after our seven-day vacation, the doctor told me that Lady was stressed by our absence. He suggested we spend about two hours with her at home, and then her hair would stick on once again. I seriously doubted the prescription, but the thought of avoiding a visit to the vet after paying the pet hotel bill worked for me. I kid you not. Within fifteen minutes of her being with us at home we couldn't pull a single hair from Lady's body. It was quite unbelievable. The doctor was right after all.

If a dog starts to fall apart after just seven days of being robbed of community, how much more is community a necessity for humans, who are created in the image of God for fellowship? We were designed by God physically, emotionally, and spiritually to require community for our health and well-being.

THE BIOCHEMISTRY OF CONNECTION

In Genesis 2:18, God tells us it was "not good" for the man he had just created to be alone. Scientific evidence now supports this idea as well: God has hardwired us for community! Allan N. Schore of the UCLA School of Medicine reports this from his extensive research: "The idea is that we are born to form attachments, that our brains are physically wired to develop in tandem with another's, through emotional communication, beginning before words are spoken."[1] In other words, our brains inextricably develop in the context of our relationships with others and their ongoing brain development. When a relationship is healthy, it imprints into our brains a resiliency against psychiatric disorders. When a relationship is unhealthy, it imprints into our brains a vulnerability to disorders.

Other studies show that males have attachment hormones,

like prolactin, which trigger us to care for our children. When we engage in care for our kids, our actions trigger the development and release of more attachment hormones, reinforcing the bonding process.[2] Researchers studying these effects conclude, "Social behavior and biology are involved in an intricate dance of mutual reinforcement."[3]

A study conducted at the Ohio State University Medical Center examined the connection between married couples and the physiological processes like immune, endocrine, and cardiovascular functioning. Researchers concluded that there is growing evidence to prove that the relationship intimacy between a husband and a wife leads "to better health, including stronger immune systems and physical wounds taking less time to heal."[4] In other words, those who lack the relational intimacy of marriage are more prone to struggle with their health. In *The Gift of Touch*, Helen Colton says that hemoglobin in the blood increases significantly when we are touched.[5] Hemoglobin is the part of the blood that carries vital supplies of oxygen to the heart and brain. She concludes that if we want to remain healthy, we must intentionally touch one another. All of these studies reinforce one fundamental truth about our need for relationships: *this is how God has made us.*

The importance of community can also be seen when we look at the behavior of the animals God has made. A 2003 study showed that rhesus monkeys that had an internal variation in one of the genes associated with serotonin seemed to be predisposed toward aggression and poor impulse control. This caused them to "binge drink" during monkey "happy hour." As a result, these monkeys were not as well-liked or accepted by the other monkeys, which led to higher rates of mortality. When monkeys with the same genetic variation that predisposes them to aggressive behavior were raised in a supportive environment, there was a surprising result. Though their genes were stacked against them, the monkeys not only survived; they thrived and rose to the top of the rhesus monkey social hierarchy! The researchers could only conclude that "an improved social environment has changed a heritable vulnerability into a positive behavioral asset."[6] They add, "Human research is pointing to a similar phenomenon."

Even beyond the findings of biochemistry and biology, researchers are uncovering evidence that the way our minds work reveals our need for community. In the past, studies have concluded that a person's intelligence was mainly based on the genetic or heritable component of IQ and that social environments had little impact.[7] But more recent scientific research is sending those earlier conclusions back to school. New studies have demonstrated that we have been wired in such a way that our social environments impact us down to the cellular level "to reduce genetically based risks" and "help substantially to raise intelligence."[8]

But you don't have to be a scientist to know that community is good for you.

Unfortunately, for many Americans, involvement in a community of healthy relationships with others is the exception, not the rule. George Gallup Jr., referring to American isolationism, writes:

> We are physically detached from each other. We change places of residence frequently. One survey revealed that seven in ten do not know their neighbors. As many as one-third of Americans admit to frequent periods of loneliness, a key factor in the high suicide rate among the elderly.[9]

Community is not a luxury; it is a necessity for life. Sadly, it is a necessity that many of us lack.

A NEW OPERATING PRINCIPLE

Remember Bob and Karen Johnson from the last chapter? The first thing Bob and Karen need to do is agree on their need to be involved in meaningful and constant community. If they can't agree on their need, they will continue to exist in their unhealthy state of loneliness and isolation. One of the underlying problems people like the Johnsons have is *too many worlds to manage*. They have too many disconnected relationships — relationships in which they do not connect at a deep level with others but which all require time and energy to maintain. Bob and Karen simply do not have enough time and energy to invest in each world's relationships in a way that allows them to find a sense of belonging and meaning for their lives.

Just think of the many disconnected worlds the Johnsons have to maintain: their own family, two places of work, church, a small group, the children's sports teams, the children's schools, extended family out of town, and neighbors. If we were to delve further into the Johnsons' lifestyle, we would discover many other worlds as well — old friends from high school and college, the last place they lived, and other relationship circles at church (for example, the women's Bible study group and the mission committee of which they are both members). On top of all this they now have online relationships, acquaintances from the past they never see but who still consider them "friends." There is a nagging sense they should be more involved in all these relationships, but they just can't seem to find the time to invest in all of them.

Prior to bringing a dog into our home, we tried to satisfy our children's longing for a pet by purchasing a hamster. The hamster seemed to spend most of its time spinning in a wheel in its cage. Often after I experienced a day filled with excessive activity but with an absence of real productivity and depth, I would look into the cage and say to myself, "At least I got more done than he did!" The hamster's central problem is a lack of anything to do; our central problem is too much to do, too much to manage. Both scenarios produce the same result: frustration. Many people today, even with so much to do compared to that hamster, experience the same thing our hamster did: *motion without meaning*.

There is no quick and easy fix to solving the problem the Johnsons and millions of Americans are experiencing. The solution does not lie simply in recommending a more meaningful activity while trying to preserve all the other worlds already in motion. If a true and workable solution is to emerge, it must involve a radical restructuring of our lifestyle. At the core of this restructuring must be a new operating principle for living. If we want a deeper sense of belonging, we must begin to consolidate our many different relational worlds into one. Like a person with multiple debts who consolidates his loans into one, we must learn to relieve ourselves of the stress of managing too many circles of relationships and focus our energy on one main circle of influence. Our mission is clear: simplify our lifestyles in such a way that we can concentrate more energy into a circle of relationships that produces a sense of genuine belonging. The goal is not to narrow our friendships or cut people out of our lives; it is to be realistic and intentional about the relationships we have, bringing depth and maturity to them.

THE ROLE OF THE CHURCH

I suggest that a local church is the best place for you and the Johnsons to go for help as you embark on this search to belong. In our postmodern age, the church is the one institution that has community built into its mission as a nonnegotiable. The mission of the church is to develop people into followers of Jesus Christ, and it takes a community to do this. The author of Hebrews lays out the priority of community, writing about "not giving up meeting together, as *some* are in the habit of doing, but encouraging one another—and all the more as you see the Day approaching."[10] The development of meaningful relationships in a community where every member carries a significant sense of belonging is central to what it means to be the church. The church is not a building; it is a God-ordained gathering of people saved by the grace of God. The purpose and calling of the church is given by God with the guarantee that even "the gates of Hades will not overcome it."[11] Yet, in the busyness of the American lifestyle, people who profess faith in Jesus Christ and do not attend church make up the largest religious category in the United States today.

If the author of Hebrews were writing his words of challenge today, he would write, "not giving up meeting together, as *most* are in the habit of doing."

My purpose in this book is not to make you feel guilty for neglecting church. Nor is it to add one more world to your already unmanageable and disconnected sets of relationships. Instead, I want to provide a vision for community, a promise of relationships with others in your church that will meet your need to belong. The Bible clearly teaches that God intends to accomplish his primary purposes in this world through his church. The first Christians understood that a decision to follow Christ also included a decision to make the church the hub of their world, even when it required the abandonment of existing social structures.

Yale University professor Wayne Meeks makes this point, based on his meticulous research of the early church: "To be 'baptized into Jesus Christ' signaled for Pauline converts an extraordinary thoroughgoing resocialization, in which the sect was intended to become virtually the primary group for its members, supplanting all other loyalties."[12] The experience of authentic community is one of the purposes God intends to be fulfilled by the church.

Some of you may have tried church and then given up on it (if not literally, then perhaps emotionally) because you were receiving a minimal return on your investment of precious time. Some of you stopped attending not because you were against church but because you found it didn't have a significant enough impact to make the short list of activities for which you had time. I suspect you may be more ambivalent toward church than against it—a reasonable attitude if you see church as merely another world to manage. Yet, as we will soon see, the Scriptures tell us that God intends the church to be the very hub at the center of one's life and community.

If the church is going to accomplish this divinely inspired purpose in a postmodern world, it will need some restructuring. In a speech to a group of pastors, Lyle Schaller, a leading church consultant over the past several decades, suggested what this restructuring might entail: "The biggest challenge for the church at the opening of the twenty-first century is to develop a solution to the discontinuity and fragmentation of the American lifestyle."[13] The church of the twenty-first century must do more than add yet another relational world to an already overbooked society; it must design new structures that help people *simplify* their lives and *develop* more meaning, depth, and purpose in their experience of community. While it is best if an entire church is engaged in this restructuring, the material in this book can take root with a small group of Christians from any local church. Those who want to connect with others in this way and become a *connecting* church must be committed to making the sacrifices needed to fully experience what God intended and created us to have. But some major and often-ignored obstacles that must be faced head-on are in the way. The next chapter introduces you to the first of these three barriers to community.

Part 1

CONNECTING TO A COMMON PURPOSE

Chapter 3

THE PROBLEM OF INDIVIDUALISM

The 1998 DreamWorks hit movie *Antz* opens with worker ant Z sitting in an ant psychiatrist's office, relating his woes of living in a modern urban ant colony. In a parody of contemporary urban life, Z (voiced by Woody Allen) says:

All my life I have lived and worked in the big city, which, now that I think of it, is a problem. Since I always feel uncomfortable around crowds — I mean I have this fear of enclosed space. Everything makes me feel trapped all the time. I always tell myself that there has to be something better out there, but maybe I think too much. I think everything must go back to the thought that I had a very anxious childhood, you know; my mother never had time for me. You know, when you're the middle child of five million you don't get any attention. I mean, how is it possible? And I have always had this abandonment issue, which plagues me. My father was basically a drone, like I've said. And, you know, he flew away when I was just a larva. And my job — don't even get me started on it because it really annoys me. I was not cut out to be a worker — I'll tell you that right now. I feel physically inadequate. My whole life I have never been able to lift more than ten times my own body weight. And when you get down to it, handling dirt, you know, is not my idea of a rewarding career. It is the whole gung-ho super organization I can't get — I have tried but I can't get it. What is it? I am supposed to be doing everything for the colony. And what about my needs? What about me? I gotta believe there is someplace out there that's better than this. Otherwise I will just curl up in a larva position and weep. The whole system makes me feel insignificant.[1]

Some of the same angst articulated by ant Z is what many urban and suburban people feel today. We want to be noticed and feel special. We want to be individuals, not just some cog in the wheel. "What about my needs?" One only needs to sign up for a social networking site to see how much of our experience of "community" today is tailored to meeting our individual needs: unique passwords, user names, pictures, desktop backgrounds, and the videos, songs, teams, groups, and games we access all attempt to make people (or, in Z's case, ants) "individuals" online.

The reflections of this urban ant exemplify a major shift in our society called *individualism*. We've been called the "me culture" by many culture specialists, and our focus on the "individual" goes beyond issues of human dignity, rights, or even the celebration of human uniqueness and diversity. All of these are valued in healthy communities. Individualism, however, is a way of life that makes the individual and his or her wants, needs, and desires *supreme* or sovereign over everything else. Individualism places a higher value on:

- lawsuits … over reconciliation
- individual rights … over community responsibilities
- career advancement … over company loyalty
- cynicism … over trust
- relative truth … over absolute truth

Individualism, where the wants and desires of the individual take precedence over all else, has no place in Christian community. For Christians, Christ is valued over all others.[2] And the Christian faith boldly and counterculturally invites us to value others more than we value ourselves.[3] Because individualism is ingrained in American culture, Bob and Karen Johnson likely haven't given it much thought, nor have they considered that it might be an obstacle in their search to belong to a meaningful, life-giving community. The Johnsons were not born into a culture of community; they were born into a culture of individualism. A culture of individualism means that when we gather in a room, we gather as a collection of individuals who are primarily concerned about our own wants and needs, not as a community united around a common cause, concern, or purpose. What makes us unique and different is more highly valued than what we have in common.

Writing in the mid-nineteenth century, Alexis de Tocqueville observed that prior societies did not even have a word for the phenomenon we now refer to as individualism, because in their time there were no individuals who did not belong to a group. The idea of being completely isolated and cut off from any form of community was inconceivable.[4] Today, it's the norm. We have become, in the words of John Locke, chairman of the Department of Human Communication Sciences at the University of Sheffield in England, "*solo* sapiens."

Most Americans tend to see individualism as a positive trait that reflects their right to exercise liberty and freedom. Individualism is seen to promote free will, free choices, free markets, and good self-esteem. Yet, after more than sixty years of trumpeting the virtues of unrestricted individualism, we are coming face-to-face with the dark side of individualism, particularly as we find ourselves increasingly lonely and isolated from one another.[5]

Locke has written about our contemporary social dysfunction in his book, *The De-Voicing of Society*. He labels our Western condition *atomization*—the fact that people today tend to drift away from each other rather than remaining connected in close-knit community. Like many sociologists and culture experts, he finds the rise of individualism dating back to post–World War II America.[6]

Peter Block, in his timely book *Community*, speaks about the danger of thinking that societal change is possible through a focus on the individual alone:

> Individual transformation is a more popular conversation, and the choice not to focus on it is because we have already

learned that the transformation of large numbers of individuals does not result in the transformation of communities. If we continue to invest in individuals as the primary target of change, we will spend our primary energy on this and never fully invest in communities. In this way, individual transformation comes at the cost of community.[7]

Individualism diminishes our sense of community. Education and culture expert E. D. Hirsch provides a list of key people, events, and literature that have helped to define America's vision, values, and purpose. He suggests that the American people should be literate about and share a common understanding of these matters. For example, Abraham Lincoln's name is on his list of key people. When Lincoln's name is mentioned, there should be shared knowledge among Americans that he was the sixteenth president of the United States. In addition to knowing this fact, an emotional response should arise concerning an important document signed by Lincoln — the Emancipation Proclamation. A bedrock value of the American society is the belief expressed in this proclamation, namely, that "all people are created equal." Hirsch strongly suggests that if we cease to share our history and a common belief as a people, we will cease to be Americans.[8] In other words, there is a huge difference between being an American and being a group of individuals who happen to reside on American soil.

Americans who were born after World War II have experienced the impact of individualism every day of their lives. Again, individualism isn't something the Johnsons chose; they were born into it. And because the Johnsons were born into it, they really have no concept of an alternative society — one based on community and rooted in common values and purposes. Because they've never experienced the alternative, they have a hard time seeing the problem with their individualism. Changes in the use of technology and the rise of social networking, e-mail, and online "communities" only make the problem of individualism worse. Online communities lack the permanence that we associate with real-world communities. If past history is any guide to the future, users tend to switch from one online community to another based on personal interest, popularity of the site, and their need at the time — from services like MySpace, to Facebook, to Twitter, to whatever is next.

The breakdown of our common beliefs and purposes has plagued not only American society but the American church as well. The "hard to swallow" premise I am making is that *today's church is not a community; it is a collection of individuals.* I don't say this to place blame on church leaders or parishioners; I simply want to describe the way things are. The pervasiveness of individualism in the church is one of the primary sources of frustration for its leaders (whether or not they identify it as individualism), and it has caused many a pastor or priest to scold their people for their lack of commitment to the church. Only now are we beginning to understand how unrealistic this call to commitment is and why it is unlikely to bear the desired fruit, given the lifestyle advocated by an individualistic culture.

After finishing his work of creation, God made only one adjustment to his original design — the addition of human community. Genesis 2 is clear that man was not made to be alone.[9] And as a reflection of how God designed us, many people, deep down, do have a longing to make a commitment to a community. But they don't know how to do it. Church leaders don't always offer solutions that encourage genuine community. Consider small groups, for example. Bob and Karen joined a church-sponsored small group, hoping to connect in community, but it didn't work for them, even laying aside their time constraints. Why not?

Like most of us, the Johnsons have brought their mind-set of individualism into their small group experience. Because their desires, expectations, and interests are based on individualistic thinking, simply joining a small group doesn't address the root problem. In fact, it contributes to the root problem because the small group itself is a dysfunctional, *individualistic* community.

The reflections of John Locke are instructive. In the final

chapter of *The De-Voicing of Society*, Locke dismantles and debunks our contemporary solutions to the problem of individualism, including small groups, pointing out how each falls short of a decisive victory. He writes:

> If small groups are thought of as a solution to desocialization, I'm afraid the news isn't very good. Few think they work, at least on a personal level ... Princeton's Robert Wuthnow has found that small groups mainly "provide occasions for individuals to focus on themselves in the presence of others. The social contract binding members together asserts only the weakest of obligations. Come if you have time. Talk if you feel like it. Respect everyone's opinion. Never criticize. Leave quietly if you become dissatisfied."
>
> In *Overcoming Loneliness in Everyday Life*, two Boston psychiatrists, Jacqueline Olds and Richard Schwartz, suggest that because of their episodic nature, groups "fail to replicate the sense of belonging we have lost. Attending weekly meetings, dropping in and out as one pleases, shopping around for a more satisfactory or appealing group—all of these factors work against the growth of true community."[10]

Robert Wuthnow probes this dysfunction further in *Sharing the Journey*.[11] He methodically presents his research on the small group movement in America and suggests that the movement initially emerged because church leaders were looking for a solution to people's longing to belong. While he concludes that the small group is an improvement over the status quo—multiple church services where people rarely talk—he also identifies a major problem with the small group experience. He identifies that most small group members do not enter the group with a common set of beliefs and purposes. Instead, everyone carries his or her own individual set of beliefs and purposes into the group. The most common response to this is to celebrate the value of each individual's right to hold whatever views they deem right and best for them. Yet, this response tends to reinforce the very value the church is seeking to address, the "unrestricted tolerance" of individualism.

If a group of people do not share common beliefs and purposes, then the highest virtue they can hold together is the toleration of the beliefs and behaviors of the other group members. Certainly there is a great need for tolerance in matters of personal style — that is, our preferences in how to raise children wisely, how to spend money responsibly, and the best route to take to get to a restaurant. But what about the lack of shared convictions on bedrock matters such as human life, human dignity, and environmental or creation management? Historically, societies (such as the Roman Empire) that failed to progress to the point of agreeing on these bedrock truths have fallen, having been destroyed from within.

Robert Wuthnow's research revealed that when the average small group member would share a particular struggle in his or her life, along with the decision on how to handle the struggle, other group members were not in a position to challenge what was shared — even if they sensed that the decision being made might harm the other person. The most common response in a group is to say nothing; the most aggressive response is to timidly suggest that this isn't the course of action they would *personally* take. Now, if the decision involves the breed of cat to purchase or the menu selection for an upcoming wedding anniversary, then a nonchallenging response is appropriate. But what if the decision is to leave a spouse, or to buy something that will put that person in massive debt, or to embrace the view that all religions have a valid path that lead to the same God? Or more realistically, what if the issue involves a strained relationship or making a career change? Applying Scripture to such practical issues is central to living as a follower of Jesus Christ, yet many small groups fail to consistently do this.

There is a big difference between a tolerant person and a codependent person. If what you and I would call destructive behavior (such as drug or alcohol abuse) is seen by the nonconfronting person as moral and not destructive, then they are considered tolerant. Live and let live. Don't rock the boat.

If what you and I would call destructive behavior *is* seen by the nonconfronting person as indeed immoral and destructive, but they actually enable that behavior despite that view, then they are considered codependent. They don't want to risk losing the person with the immoral or destructive behavior from their life, so they help to make that behavior possible.

Are our small group relationships merely tolerant, or are they — even worse — codependent when they are faced with members who are thinking about or actually engaging in immoral or destructive behavior? Or are those relationships based on a set of shared, mutual convictions about what leads to thriving, healthy relationships so that the members can hold one another truly accountable? The Christian faith offers a basic set of beliefs, values, practices, and virtues essential for a constructive and fruitful life. The Word of God is powerful to effect change and transformation in the lives of people, but it must be applied in our relationships, a practice that rubs against our ingrained cultural individualism. Consider the words of the apostle Peter:

> [God's] divine power has given us everything we need for a godly life through our knowledge of him who called us by his own glory and goodness. Through these he has given us his very great and precious promises, so that through them you may participate in the divine nature, having escaped the corruption in the world caused by evil desires.
>
> For this very reason, make every effort to add to your faith goodness; and to goodness, knowledge; and to knowledge, self-control; and to self-control, perseverance; and to perseverance, godliness; and to godliness, mutual affection; and to mutual affection, love. For if you possess these qualities in increasing measure, they will keep you from being ineffective and unproductive in your knowledge of our Lord Jesus Christ. But whoever does not have them is nearsighted and blind, forgetting that they have been cleansed from their past sins.
>
> Therefore, my brothers and sisters, make every effort to

confirm your calling and election. For if you do these things, you will never stumble, and you will receive a rich welcome into the eternal kingdom of our Lord and Savior Jesus Christ.[12]

In this passage, we find a basic and essential set of beliefs, values, practices, and virtues set out for us, which still leave room for disagreement on the nonessentials. As Robert Wuthnow has suggested, one of the major problems with the typical small group in America is that people do not enter the group with a common understanding and commitment to the basic tenets of the Christian faith. They may acknowledge that their church has a doctrinal statement of beliefs, but often they do not understand the relationship of these beliefs to daily life and therefore are not really committed to them for everyday living. These beliefs, which form the bedrock of Christian identity and practice, have no practical influence in the small group. Instead, everyone has their own individual idea or opinion as to what the Christian life is all about.

Many people assume that the churched Christian has a firm handle on the biblical theology that fuels the Christian life. Yet, an extensive Barna Research Group study has shown that "Americans' Bible knowledge is in the ballpark, but often off base."[13] Surveys have found that Americans have strongly held theological positions but that these positions often conflict with biblical views. The greatest challenge for churches may be dealing with the fact that most of its adults only *think* they have both extensive and accurate Bible knowledge.

So the question before us is this: Can a group of Christians who do not share a common set of beliefs, practices, and virtues really be considered a Christian community, or are they just a group of individuals who happen to gather together on "Christian soil"? This is something to ponder. We're not talking about people who do not attend a church. These are people who claim to embrace Christ as their Savior and the Son of God. They simply don't know how the Christian life works.

Dallas Willard, professor at the University of Southern

California's School of Philosophy, offers the observation that by the middle of the twentieth century, the church had "lost any recognized, reasonable, theologically and psychologically sound approach to spiritual growth, to really becoming like Christ."[14] As we have seen, one of the chief ingredients of individualism is the rejection, consciously or unconsciously, of the notion that there is a common set of beliefs that should bind "me" to others. This rejection presents one of the greatest obstacles we face in overcoming the plague of individualism. Many in our culture today believe that adherence to a common set of beliefs, traditions, or doctrines only leads to the abuse of power, a form of brainwashing that inhibits the free expression of our personal tastes and creativity.

I suggest the church must thoughtfully challenge the current view that prioritizes the individual over all else. Though it runs against the grain of our culture, we must be committed to the truth, even when it is not popular. In his gospel, John introduces the coming of Jesus with these words: "For the law was given through Moses; grace and truth came through Jesus Christ."[15] Jesus always deals with us in *truth* but does so graciously.

Jesus tells us we are sinners — those who have offended God — and he says it because it's true. Hearing this may be, and certainly was in Jesus' day, offensive to some. But in his relationships with others, Jesus always spoke on the basis of truth. When Jesus met the woman at the well in Samaria, he confronted her with the truth of her failed marriages and current "live-in" situation.[16] When he dealt with the woman caught in adultery who was about to be stoned by a group of hypocritical men, he identified her actions as sinful.[17]

In contrast to the religious leaders of his day, however, Jesus tells us the truth in a way that is filled with grace. For sinners, Jesus Christ graciously died on the cross to pay the debt we owed for our sins. For the Samaritan woman at the well, he offered "living water" as a real solution to her broken life. For the woman caught in adultery, he rescued her from a lynch mob by creatively chasing them away.

For Jesus, grace without truth is not real grace—it's a lie that is ultimately destructive and harmful to the person. Yet, truth without grace is no better—it fails to offer hope that change is possible. The alternative to our contemporary tolerance is to do what Jesus did—dealing with others in "grace and truth." As Christians, we must learn to uphold the basic elements of the Christian faith as revealed in the Bible while faithfully dispensing this truth in a gracious way.

To do what Jesus did should go a long way toward preventing spiritual abuse and legalism. The apostle Paul confirmed the teaching and practice of Jesus by saying we should speak the truth in love.[18] Whenever this takes place in Christian community, "the whole body, joined and held together by every supporting ligament, grows and builds itself up in love, as each part does its work."[19]

While this may not be the experience of the majority of Christian churches or small groups at present, it can be achieved. The prevailing mind-set of individualism is a serious obstacle to community. It was for the Johnsons, and it may well be for you too! But it doesn't have to be.

Chapter 4

CHARACTERISTICS OF A COMMON PURPOSE

The church has become a collection of individuals, due at least in part to the prevailing mind-set of individualism in our culture. In this chapter, I offer what I see as the principal solution to overcoming the devastating effects of individualism on our search to belong. The answer is simple and straightforward: *we must have a common purpose.* We must once again come together around a set of shared beliefs and values. Bob and Karen must become a part of such a community, or their search will continue indefinitely.

Based on his extensive research of the social world of the first-century church, historian Wayne Meeks has written, "One peculiar thing about early Christianity was the way in which the intimate, close-knit life of the local groups was seen to be simultaneously part of a much larger, indeed ultimately worldwide, movement or entity."[1] At a basic level, community unites us to a purpose bigger than our own lives as individuals. I propose that communities united around a common purpose share five characteristics.

FIVE CHARACTERISTICS OF COMMUNITY AROUND A COMMON PURPOSE

The principle of sharing a common purpose is not new; it is an ancient principle that must be rediscovered. Its presence is simply not optional if you want true community. If you were to study places where community exists, you would find the embodiment of certain characteristics that uphold a common purpose. What are these characteristics?

Authority

In a community united around a common purpose we find a clear understanding of and respect for the authority structure. Someone is responsible to lead the community in such a way that it upholds and advances the common purpose. It is this authority structure that blesses and reinforces positive behavior and holds community members accountable for negative or destructive behavior. In the typical American Christian small group, we love to use the word *accountability*. But if we are precise in our definitions, we really don't have accountability; we only have *disclosure*. A group member is often willing to disclose personal struggles and decisions, but there usually is no invitation to challenge the choices or to hold the person accountable to an objective standard.

True accountability calls for the appropriate and wise use of authority and leverage. If a group today seeks to exercise authority over a member who is pursuing an unacceptable standard (for example, an unbiblical divorce or a marriage to a non-Christian), this member will very likely simply leave the group. Because most people don't want him or her to leave, the member's actions and attitudes are never challenged. Often, the destructive actions or the disintegration of a relationship are not even known by the other members until it's too late to step in and lovingly address the situation.

In the Old Testament nomadic community of Abraham, it was clear that Abraham was the authority, the patriarch. In the first-century church of Jerusalem, the authority was Peter. In the first-century culture, the head of the household was responsible for the nuclear family (the *oikos*), and all aspects of society supported this structure. Wayne Meeks writes, "The head of the household, by normal expectations of the society, would exercise some authority over the group and would have some legal responsibility for it. The structure of the *oikos* was hierarchical, and contemporary political and moral thought regarded the structure of superior and inferior roles as basic to the well-being of the whole society."[2]

In an Amish community, there is a head elder, who is respected and who has authority to watch over and administer the values and beliefs of the community. In the tight-knit community of a monastery, the abbot (meaning "father") guides the monks toward their ultimate purpose of achieving union with God. Even gangs, which have emerged in large part because of a lack of healthy public places in which community can be experienced, have a clearly established leader. Their purpose may be a destructive purpose, but the purpose is clear and the authority is in place.

But can this kind of authority structure and accountability really work in American culture? Yes, but it will require us to challenge the assumptions and values people bring with them when they come to Christ. It will require the church to operate as a countercultural community. Given our culture of individualism, we should remember that all the characteristics of community are countercultural in some way. So some form of authority will be needed for healthy community in a church. While abuses must be guarded against, abandoning authority altogether is not a workable solution.

In 2003, a couple of years after the first edition of *The Connecting Church* was published, a study was commissioned to recommend solutions for the rise of "at risk" children in the United States. The study concluded our children had never been better off economically, but at the same time, they had never been worse off emotionally, mentally, and behaviorally. The study revealed:

- One in four adolescents in the United States was at serious risk of not achieving productive adulthood.
- Children in the early twenty-first century reported higher

levels of anxiety than did children who were psychiatric patients in the 1950s.

- One in five students had seriously considered suicide in the past year.
- One in three teenagers reported engaging in binge drinking.[3]

The study's conclusion strongly suggested that more psycho-therapy and medications would not help. The only sustainable, global, and transformational solution would be to return to our children what they had—and have—lost. So what has been lost? The researchers coined a new phrase to describe it: "authoritative community."[4]

The report reads as follows:

> Our choice of the word "authoritative" comes after consider-able reflection, especially since we are concerned that readers of the report, and members of the public who may hear about it, might confuse "authoritative" with "authoritarian," a word which is commonly associated with a largely coercive ("com-mand control") approach to raising children and relating to others. We are eager to avoid that confusion. But we believe that the word "authoritative" is worth reclaiming and using. The word refers to a strong body of scholarly evidence dem-onstrating the value of the particular combination of warmth and structure in which children in a democratic society appear most likely to thrive.[5]

As much as we may recoil at the idea of authority as a posi-tive aspect of community, the truth is that our kids are dying for it. Why? Because authority is one of the core characteristics of a healthy community.

Common Creed

Another characteristic of effective communities of purpose is a common creed, a shared understanding of the beliefs and prac-tices that guide the community. For a twelve-step group, this would be the twelve steps themselves; for the children of Israel, it was the Law.

Throughout the centuries, the Christian church has sensed the need for and importance of establishing common creeds. Historian Wayne Meeks observes that in the first-century urban church, it was not just "shared content of beliefs but also shared forms by which the beliefs are expressed [that] are important in promoting cohesiveness. Every close-knit group develops its own argot, and the use of that argot in speech among members knits them more closely still."[6] Martin Luther, one of the great Protestant Reformers, felt compelled to create a common creed in the 1500s. The Augsburg Confession, written by Luther's friend and colleague Philipp Melanchthon, laid out the twenty-one articles of faith that guide the beliefs and practices of the Lutheran Church. After visiting some of the churches and realizing that the Confession had not made its way to the pew, Luther wrote a "smaller" catechism comprised of questions and answers pertaining to the Ten Commandments, the Apostles' Creed, and the Lord's Prayer.

John Calvin, another great Reformation leader, developed the Geneva Catechism for the Reformed Church in 1536. The Religious Society of Friends (Quakers) developed a creed in the 1600s. The Roman Catholic Church published a creed from the Council of Trent in 1566, known as the Roman Catechism. In 1885, a new creed for Catholics was published in America, called the Baltimore Catechism. The Church of England has the Book of Common Prayer, divided into two parts — the first explains the baptismal covenant, the Apostles' Creed, the Ten Commandments, and the Lord's Prayer, while the second explains the sacraments of baptism and the Eucharist. In 1646, the Presbyterians developed the Westminster Confession of Faith.

For the past sixty years, the American church has lacked a common creed. Declining mainline denominational churches may still retain their confessional creeds, but they often carry little meaning for the majority of their members. And for the most part, the fast-growing contemporary church lacks any connection to a historical creed or confession. The litmus test for any church is to randomly ask members to articulate the common creed that binds them together. In most cases, the response will be a blank stare. Again, this reality points to the challenge of individualism: We do not see the value in a common belief structure. And yet every effective community will share a common creed.

Traditions

A true community uses traditions to perpetuate the purpose and pass them on to the people of that community, particularly to the children. Traditions are things you always do in the same manner and perhaps at the same time that hold great value in communicating meaning to the people of the community. A tradition can be a symbol or festival or any activity that reinforces the beliefs, values, practices, virtues, and purposes of a community.

On a military base, for example, a long and carefully perfected list of traditions has been put in place to remember a significant event, to communicate an important military value, or to honor a soldier who exemplifies military values. Awards ceremonies for heroism are chock-full of rich tradition. Each badge, medal, or stripe represents particular deeds and is given out by a particular person in authority in a particular way. The military funeral is another event defined by tradition. The presentation of the neatly triangular-folded American flag to the next of kin and the twenty-one-gun salute are just two traditions that communicate honor, community, and meaning.

The people of Israel had built-in traditions, such as Passover, the Feast of Booths, Hanukkah, the Year of Jubilee, and the like, to recount God's faithfulness and to instruct the community in the principles of the Law. Tradition was the central means of passing on the faith to the next generation. Consider these words recorded by Moses:

> "In the future, when your son asks you, 'What is the meaning of the stipulations, decrees and laws the Lord our God has commanded you?' tell him: 'We were slaves of Pharaoh in

Egypt, but the LORD brought us out of Egypt with a mighty hand. Before our eyes the LORD sent signs and wonders—great and terrible—on Egypt and Pharaoh and his whole household. But he brought us out from there to bring us in and give us the land he promised on oath to our ancestors. The LORD commanded us to obey all these decrees and to fear the LORD our God, so that we might always prosper and be kept alive, as is the case today. And if we are careful to obey all this law before the LORD our God, as he has commanded us, that will be our righteousness.'"[7]

For the first-century church, Jesus established Communion, or the Eucharist, to remember his death until he comes again.[8] And as one reads the book of Acts, it's clear how important baptism was to the early church.

Just as a culture of individualism scorns a common creed, it holds disdain for tradition. While some traditions clearly need to be reevaluated, and done away with on occasion, all places of true community have them as an important part of life together. To be sure, there is a difference between traditionalism and traditions. Traditionalism expresses the dead faith of the living; tradition expresses the living faith of the dead. If we are to rediscover community, we must revitalize old, or create new, traditions that impart our purposes, values, and beliefs and influence our thinking.

Standards

Another characteristic found in places of community is the presence of standards, a list of written or unwritten guidelines that define what is expected of the community's people. These standards lay out what is considered acceptable behavior. For example, in a traditional Amish community, marriage to an outsider is condemned, and members of the community are expected to wear plain clothing with hooks and eyes as fasteners instead of buttons. If you had lived in a Benedictine monastery at any time in the last fourteen hundred years, you would be very familiar with the seventy-three chapters of the Rule of St. Benedict, which lay out the standards for living in the monastery. The rule book details everything from showing reverence at prayer to instructions on how monks are to sleep.

Community standards have formed a basis for communal life from the beginning of time, and yet here, too, our culture of individualism resists the idea of common standards. We resist the idea that there is a "right way" to live. We resist the notion of rules or laws, seeing them as potential obstacles to our self-fulfillment. This is why we need to rediscover the importance of standards for healthy community. The Commission on Children at Risk recognizes the value of standards, strongly recommending that if we are to turn the tide in the emotional, mental, and behavioral decline of our children, we must create communities for them that "model and pass on at least part of what it means to be a good person and live a good life."[9]

We want community, but few seem open to the characteristics that promote it and sustain its life. If we want community, we must factor in this countercultural practice of following standards.

Common Mission

Any true community will have a clearly defined mission that brings the individuals of a group together and knits them into a cohesive family. For the military platoon sharing a foxhole, the mission could be to secure a town, blow up a bridge, take a hill, or protect a dignitary. For an Amish community, it is the preservation of a way of life and separation from the negative effects of modern-day culture. For a recovery group, it is freedom from addiction. So powerful is the sense of common mission in drawing people together that M. Scott Peck calls the recovery group one of the most effective places of community today. When you come across a place of community that truly works, you will discover that its members share a common mission that is larger than any one person.

THE COMMON PURPOSE OF CHRISTIAN COMMUNITY

Having a common purpose is precisely what made the first-century church in Jerusalem so dynamic. Luke records these words in Acts: "All the believers were together, but they all had their own ideas as to why they were there." Wait a minute. That's not what it says! The verse reads, "All the believers were together and had everything in common."[10] Do you wonder what that means? Just two verses before, Luke says that the believers "devoted themselves to the apostles' teaching and to fellowship, to the breaking of bread and to prayer"[11] — in other words, to a distinct set of beliefs and practices. They did this together. They were all on the same page; they had a common purpose. Later, Luke tells us that "all the believers were one in heart and mind."[12]

Notice that the Bible says *all*, not just some, came together in Christian community around one set of beliefs and convictions that were leading to a distinct set of actions and behaviors. In establishing a theology for Christian community, the apostle Paul writes, "There is one body and one Spirit — just as you were called to one hope when you were called — one Lord, one faith, one baptism; one God and Father of all, who is over all and through all and in all."[13] The distinct impression here is that embracing a common belief and purpose built on the teachings of Jesus and the apostles was, and still is, a requirement for being called a Christian community.

Most churches today have not been able to rally around a common purpose. Lyle Schaller, a leading church consultant, writes, "Rising from the debris of our lost values is the new value on the individual. The 'me' generation has given way to a 'me' world. The question is, how will the church, the ultimate 'we' organization, adjust?"[14] Kenneth Kantzer, former professor and dean at Trinity Evangelical Divinity School, made this prophetic statement based on his study of the modern church: "No church can be effective to bring clarity and commitment to a world when it is as ignorant of its own basic principles as is our church today. And unless we engage the church in a mighty program of reeducation, it will be unable to transmit a Christian heritage to its own children or to the society around it."[15]

One of the most important writers of the twentieth century, C. S. Lewis, helps identify the common cause Christians should be committed to:

> [Christ] works on us in all sorts of ways ... But above all, He works on us through each other. Men are mirrors, or "carriers" of Christ to other men ... Usually it is those who know Him that bring Him to others. That is why the Church, the whole body of Christians showing Him to one another, is so important.... It is easy to think that the Church has a lot of different objects—education, building, missions, holding services ... *The Church exists for no other purpose but to draw men into Christ, to make them little Christs.* If they are not doing that, all the cathedrals, clergy, missions, sermons, even the Bible itself, are simply a waste of time. God became Man for no other purpose. It is even doubtful, you know, whether the whole universe was created for any other purpose.[16]

Jesus himself gave us the mission to "make disciples" of people and to obey his entire teachings. Paul states it this way: "My dear children, for whom I am again in the pains of childbirth until Christ is formed in you ..."[17]

What the church urgently needs is to reconnect to its core mission of making disciples. We need to get back to the basics: Why did God create the church? Why does the church even exist? As a community of Jesus followers, we must learn to see that our corporate mandate is "to be Jesus" to each other and to the world. As the one body of Christ, we await the second coming of Jesus himself, but until that day we are called to represent his presence, his purposes, and fulfill his plans in the power of the Holy Spirit.

To do this, we must be formed, progressively, more and more into his image, seeking to become like the One we follow. And to accomplish this, the church must define, as Dallas Willard has suggested, a "recognized, reasonable, theologically and psychologically sound approach to spiritual growth," or Christ forming.[18]

We should adopt from the ancient church and redefine for the postmodern church what a follower of Christ looks like today. We must seek a way of incorporating our common beliefs, practices, and virtues into the lives of people so that collectively we can represent Jesus to others and fulfill our purpose of making disciples formed into his image.

A word of caution here: the church must be careful not to confuse an assimilation strategy for church involvement with a spiritual formation model for community building. Both are necessary, but they are very different. An assimilation strategy defines how one gets involved in the life and programs of a church; a spiritual formation model defines the essential outcomes the church is attempting to get working into the lives of its members. Church leaders should first define the end objective for their people and then design an infrastructure to accomplish this in the lives of the people of the church. To have an effective assimilation strategy that will get people involved in the church but then to not have a clear idea of what the ultimate purpose of those structures are would be hollow and aimless. The Bible does not define church activities as "spiritual formation"; rather, spiritual growth involves the "renewing of the mind" in the core beliefs of the Christian faith.[19]

Central beliefs that forge our communion with God—such as our belief in the Trinity, salvation by grace, the authority of the Bible, the personal nature of God, and our identity in Christ—are a necessity. Central beliefs that cement our communion with people—such as our view of the church, biblical humanity, Christian compassion, eternity, and biblical stewardship—must be considered.

Spiritual growth involves practicing the ancient disciplines taught in the Bible and experienced throughout church history.[20] Christian disciplines that foster our relationship with God—such as worship, prayer, Bible study, and single-mindedness—should also be included. The biblical practices of community, spiritual gifts, and giving away our time, money, faith, and even our life are also needed to help us fulfill the royal law of loving our neighbor.

Of course, in all of our efforts we must not forget the basis of our spiritual formation—the character of Christ.[21] The end goal of a life formed in the Spirit is a life that bears the fruit of the Spirit: love, joy, peace, forbearance, kindness, goodness, faithfulness, gentleness, and self-control.[22] These virtues define a mature disciple.

If Bob and Karen Johnson are going to satisfy their longing for more intimate relationships, they must find, and even help create, a Christian community where the common mission is to see individuals become actively developing followers of Christ who, in turn, are committed to living out their new life for the sake of others as Christ did. This community must have in place respected spiritual authority—individuals who are biblically literate and who can serve as exemplary spiritual mentors. This gathering must have a common creed that succinctly lays out the beliefs, practices, and virtues the members of the community agree to follow, encourage in each other, and to which they all are held accountable. They must resurrect old, or create new, Christian traditions that assist in cementing the history and purpose of the Christian faith for the next generation. And, if this community is to be effective in the long term, there must be standards that are considered acceptable behavior for all followers of Christ.

Notice how Paul challenges the mind-set of individualism. If any of these characteristics are absent, the authenticity of the community will in some way be diminished:

> If you have any encouragement from being united with Christ, if any comfort from his love, if any common sharing in the Spirit, if any tenderness and compassion, then make my joy complete by being like-minded, having the same love, being one in spirit and of one mind. Do nothing out of selfish ambition or vain conceit. Rather, in humility value others above yourselves, not looking to your own interests but each of you to the interests of the others.

In your relationships with one another, have the same mindset as Christ Jesus.[23]

Whatever our particular model of spiritual formation, it should be promoted by the spiritual authority of the church, be taught at all levels, form a common language that people of the community use to speak with each other, and be the benchmark against which we examine our lives as individuals and as a community.[24]

How are we, as the church, doing today? Dallas Willard suggests that most churches aren't effectively making disciples:

> The fact is that our existing churches and denominations do not have active, well-designed, intently pursued plans to accomplish this in their members. Just as you will not find any national leader today who has a plan for paying off the national debt; so you will not find any widely influential element of our church leadership that has a plan — not a vague wish or dream, but a plan — for implementing all phases of the Great Commission.[25]

Church leaders should ask themselves, "What is our plan for teaching our people to obey everything Christ has commanded?" A common purpose as defined by Scripture itself is what Bob and Karen — and all of us — need if we are going to experience Christian community. In the next chapter, I'll do my best to lay out the biblical purpose God has in mind for us as his church, the community of those who follow Jesus.

Chapter 5

REDISCOVERING BIBLICAL PURPOSE

Bob and Karen Johnson have been attending church services and church-sponsored activities for a while but have not had the opportunity to become part of a community of Christians focused on the same, rich biblical purpose. This is true not only for the Johnsons but for most Christians today. As Dallas Willard puts it, paraphrasing G. K. Chesterton, "It's not so much that the Christian life has been tried and found wanting as it's never been tried at all."[1] What follows is one example of what a community of faith looks like when people are invited and equipped to experience their God-given purpose.

GOD'S STORY

For the Johnsons to discover their authentic biblical purpose, both as individuals and as a family, they must first be invited to look beyond their own stories to see God's story. They begin by asking these questions: Who is God? What is he doing? What is his purpose and driving passion?

Let's start with a question and a statement about God's *identity*. Who is God?

He is the one true God, whose nature is a community—Father, Son, and Holy Spirit.

Orthodox Christianity spent several centuries working hard to get this right. Understanding who God is—his nature—is essential to our understanding of God's self-identity, his purposes, and his passions. In this statement we identify the mystery of the Trinity: God is *one* yet *three*, and he is *three* yet *one*. This concept immediately upsets our individualistic ways of thinking because most of us have never thought outside of the box in this way. To our way of thinking, one equals one, and that's the end of the story. We can hardly conceive of a perfect unity of multiple persons because all we know is existence defined by our individualism.

The challenging implications of this statement are nothing new, and when the early church began teaching the idea of the Trinity, it immediately invited controversy. In the first three hundred years after Christ, as the church grew and spread, thoughtful Christian thinkers studied the Scriptures and concluded that the teaching of God's tri-personal unity reveals something wonderful and mysterious about our own existence.

The study of our existence—or our "being"—is called *ontology*. And as thinkers studied the Bible, they saw that God is made up of three distinct persons—Father, Son, and Holy Spirit—yet each one of these persons is fully God. Collectively, they concluded this meant that the three persons are joined together in such a way as to form one *being*. In other words, God is a social God, a relational self.[2]

Wrapping your mental arms around this idea may give you a headache! Believe me, though, it is well worth the time and effort required. Understanding the nature of God as a community of persons is important because the Bible tells us we are made in the image of this God. So if you want to understand how God has designed you, you first need to understand the makeup of God himself. Imagine, if you will, three people squeezing into a hula hoop—yes, that plastic cylinder apparatus popularized by Wham-O in the 1950s that swings around gyrating hips. Each person in this hoop can be clearly identified as a whole and distinct person. We can recognize each of them and call them by their name and have a conversation with them individually. These three persons are unique yet are all contained in a single, shared ring as a community. The ring they share in common is called their "being" or "essence." Unlike the mere joining of individuals, our God is one being, *existing* as three persons.

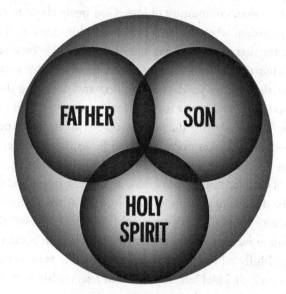

What this means is that community is not just something God thinks is a good idea; it is the way his very being and nature are expressed. The Bible tells us that God is love.[3] And for love to exist, there must necessarily be a relationship of persons in which it can be expressed. Love requires a community.

Within the Trinity, we see the perfect community, perfectly exhibiting the fruit of the Spirit in their unified relationship. There is perfect "love, joy, peace, forbearance, kindness, goodness, faithfulness, gentleness and self-control."[4] What a wonderful place to belong! It certainly doesn't get any better than this.

Knowing that God's self-identity is relational—that God is a relational being, a community of three persons—helps us to better understand God's passion and his purposes. As we read the first two chapters of Genesis, God's passion becomes clear. The point of God's act of creation was not to win the blue ribbon at the intergalactic science fair, though it would certainly be well-deserved. No, God desired to express the beauty of his eternal relationships, the love expressed between the Father, Son, and Holy Spirit, by making creatures in his own image and likeness. Out of the overflow of his own community of love, God freely chose to create a place, a garden, where he could meet with his creation. Then he formed the first man out of the dust of the earth. He breathed into Adam's nostrils, and Adam came to life. Amazing! But something was not right. After six days of creating and declaring the work was good, God said it was *not good* for the man to be alone in the garden. To remedy this dilemma, God—Father, Son, and Holy Spirit—said, "'Let *us* make mankind in our own image, in our likeness ...' So God created mankind in his own image, in the image of God he created them; male and female he created them."[5]

The divine community of God looking at the divinely made community of people saw that it was "very good."[6] Why? Because once Adam was put into community with another human being, mankind fully reflected the image of God. The man was no longer just an individual but was united in relationship with another person, one who was different yet shared a common essence. The being of humans now reflected the being of God as a community of persons, and they became "one flesh."[7] They shared a hula hoop.

God's passion was, and is, to see his community of eternal love multiply. His desire was to be in relationship with his people in the garden world he had made for them. But as the story continues, we see that Adam and Eve didn't embrace this vision. They chose to disobey God, breaking fellowship with him and with one another. Sin, the expression of our individualistic selfishness, became second nature for Adam and Eve. Instead of acting for the good of God and others, for their blessing and benefit, they now acted for their own good alone. They possessed the knowledge of good and evil, the good they had lost and the evil they had chosen. Their actions following their sin reflected their selfishness. Instead of loving one another in imitation of the Trinity, they blamed each other. And their sin, like a virus, was passed on to their children as well.

The chapters that follow record a story of a jealous brother who, after God rejects his sacrifice—the fruit of his labors—chooses to kill his brother. Rather than celebrate with his brother, Abel, and take pleasure in him—a mark of Trinitarian love ("This is my Son, whom I love; with him I am well pleased"[8]), Cain nurses his bruised ego and allows bitter jealousy to reign in his heart.

The story line falters. Death and destruction seem victorious as Adam and Eve are escorted out of the garden, away from God's presence. Abel is killed. Cain is exiled, destined to a nomadic life. There is no one left in the hula hoop. Through sin, individualism as a way of life is born.

But the story is not over yet. God refuses to give up, and he establishes a rescue plan to win back the hearts of those he has made, to free them from their selfishness and individualism. God provides a way—the *only* way to restore the community lost through sin—by offering the Son as payment for our sins. This wasn't a plan forced on the Son. As a member of the Trinity, the community of God's eternal love, he willingly took on this assignment, knowing it was the only way to satisfy the justice and mercy of God.[9] The Bible tells us this act of selfless sacrifice by the Trinity is the ultimate expression of love. In fact, every other story in the Bible from Genesis 3 through Revelation is intended to unfold a dimension of this great plan of God, his masterful design to rescue and restore his people.

How does the story end? What is the desired outcome? God's *vision* was to come down to be with us in the garden. And in the end, his vision is accomplished in Jesus Christ. As God's saved people, we will one day be with him as he comes down to be with us in a *new* garden on a *new*, restored earth. Those who accept by faith the grace of Christ's offer of forgiveness see the consequences of Adam's decision overturned and the promises restored to them in Christ.[10] They will receive new bodies, unshackled from sin, and will dwell with God in the new garden forever and ever.[11] From garden to a garden city, the Bible begins and ends with a vision of God in the presence of his people. Through the sacrifice of the Son, God pursues, rescues, and restores his people, accomplishing the great passion of his heart: to dwell with his people, to be with them, living together in fellowship and community.

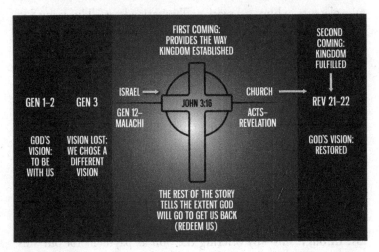

The vision of God is not about you or about me; it's about *us!* God's passion and his purpose is that we would live in community with him and with one another. Community is not just a means to an end for God; it is the end in itself. Until Bob and Karen catch a vision for the importance of community, they will never be able to see beyond their own individualistic needs, wants, and desires. And if they fail to grasp this vision, they will certainly never pass it on to their two children.[12] As a family, they need to realign their lives to this grand direction, the story of the ages.

OUR STORY

Yet it's not quite that simple, is it? There is something still missing from all of this. Before the Johnsons can move from God's story to their own individual purpose, they need to grasp the story that lies in between — "our story." As followers of Jesus, we providentially find ourselves living in the era of the church between his first and second comings. The church is a new community of people who have placed their faith in Jesus and are committed to living out his mission under his kingdom rule. As Christians, our identity, passion, strategy, and purpose originate with God. Our aim is to align our life as the church to the plans of God.

So, what is *our* identity as the people of God? When we place our faith and our life in Christ for salvation, God instantly and automatically places us in a community with others he has saved, a community called the church. Though we maintain our identities as unique people, collectively we make up a new, unified, single body — the body of Christ.[13]

In this community, we are called to experience a taste of the unity the Son has with the Father.[14] As Adam and Eve were called to represent the image of God in the garden prior to the fall, together we are now called to represent the image of God to the world. And because this image is primarily communal in nature (as we saw in Genesis 1), the restoration of this image must also be communal.

In Colossians 3:9 – 10, Paul writes: "Do not lie to each other, since you have taken off your old self with its practices and have put on the new self, which is being renewed in knowledge in the image of its Creator." Here we see evidence of what it means to "restore" the image of God that we share in communal life with others. Outside of the hula hoop of life in God's community of love, we did not produce the fruit of the Spirit. We lied, cheated, and related to one another in sin and selfishness.[15] But when we placed our faith in Christ, we entered a whole new way of life — life with other redeemed folks from every walk of life. The new self Paul refers to is one that reflects the likeness of Jesus Christ. It's a relational self, one that is being renewed in the image of its Creator. This renewed image refuses to live in selfishness and isolation from others. It seeks to love others the way God loves.

Because this community was first reflected in the marriage of the man and the woman, it makes sense it is first restored in that relationship. In fact, in his letter to the Ephesians, Paul gives us a clue into the redeemed and restored purpose of marriage — that it serves as a pointer to the relationship between Christ and his church:

> After all, no one ever hated their own body, but they feed and care for their body, just as Christ does the church—for we are members of his body. "For this reason a man will leave his father and mother and be united to his wife, and the two will become one flesh." This is a profound mystery—but I am talking about Christ and the church.[16]

This is a mind-blowing concept, if we are willing to accept it. Paul takes us back to Genesis 2 and informs us that the declaration of marriage between Adam and Eve was a picture of the unity God intends for his church, in her relationship with her Savior, Jesus Christ. As part of that unity, we are members of one body. Rather than hating our body, we feed it and care for it. Our "it" becomes "we" as we learn to love those who are part of this new community of love.

As the body of Christ, our passion is to *be* the presence of Christ on earth until his return. We are to represent his *presence*, live out his *plan*, and fulfill his *promise* in the *power* of the Holy Spirit within us. Jesus tells us that "where two or three gather in my name, there am I with them."[17] When believers gather together physically around the purposes of Jesus, it is just as though he is there with them in the room. Jesus tells us we represent him as we go into the world to do the things he has asked us to do, and he promises to be with us every step of the way until the very end.[18]

Jesus commissioned his disciples, huddled in fear in the upper room, to go downstairs and swing open the front door. He asked them to leave behind their fears and boldly be his witnesses, starting in Jerusalem and then moving out to Judea and to Samaria and to the ends of the earth. Jesus didn't want his presence hidden in the upper room or contained in the back room of the temple. He wanted to be on the move through us. God's passion for his people, as the body of Christ, is that we take his life-transforming presence to every neighborhood and nation, every nook and cranny, every corner and crevice of this dark world.

Our command is not to *go to* church" but to "*be* the church." Our marching orders are not "come and see" but "go and be." We are not to hide our light under the bushel of a church building but let it shine out in the community. The life of Christ is a cure for the sickness that ails the human race, the disease that ravages our lives, and the sin that leads to spiritual and physical death. As Christ followers *in community*, we carry the cure of Jesus wherever we go. This is *who* we are and *what* we are to be about. God's story gives us our identity and our passion.

So, what is God's strategy for accomplishing his purposes in us, his people? Acts 2:42 – 47 gives insight into how the early church understood and implemented the commission given by Jesus in Matthew 28 and Acts 1. The first believers gathered in homes in Jerusalem. After Peter's first sermon, three thousand joined the initial 120 believers. Historians tell us that each house church likely contained somewhere around thirty people.[19] If this is so, then roughly more than a hundred gatherings were sprinkled throughout Jerusalem in those early days. Imagine what it would have been like to be at one of the house church meetings. Here is a description of what it was like:

> They devoted themselves to the apostles' teaching and to fellowship, to the breaking of bread and to prayer. Everyone was filled with awe at the many wonders and signs performed by the apostles. All the believers were together and had everything in common. They sold property and possessions to give to anyone who had need. Every day they continued to meet together in the temple courts. They broke bread in their homes and ate together with glad and sincere hearts, praising God and enjoying the favor of all the people. And the Lord added to their number daily those who were being saved.[20]

Another way of saying this is that the believers who made up the body of Christ in a particular neighborhood devoted themselves to *belonging*. Basic fellowship was a core priority of this small community of Christ followers. The primary way they expressed their belonging to Christ and to one another was in a meal. As a matter of fact, the entire church service was centered on this shared evening meal.[21] The table of the Lord's Supper became the visible expression of their life together—a sign for all to see that there was a new community based on the shared life they enjoyed through God's Spirit, in turn based on the Son's sacrifice and the Father's adoption.

As followers of Christ, they devoted themselves to *growing*—in a lifelong journey to look more like Christ together as his body.[22] To facilitate this, they devoured the teaching of the apostles, sitting back and loosening the ropes on their robes to recline around the dinner table after a scrumptious meal. The apostles' teaching reconnected and resocialized them for life in a different kind of community, a community based not on selfish patterns of sin but on the life of love in the community of the Trinity. God's Word instructed them how to love God, how to love one another, and how to love their neighbors—those around them who did not yet know the good news about God's salvation.

They were a people passionate about *praying*. In praying together, they connected vertically with the community of the Godhead. They prayed to know God, to discover his will for their lives together, and to lay their requests before him. Their lives were radically changed through these times of prayer, creating an awe in their hearts—a sense of wonder, respect, and amazement at what God was doing in their midst. They were together, and they had everything in common.

Out of the overflow of their lives together and stirring of the Holy Spirit within them, they began *serving* each other and the people around them. They made it a priority to care for one another as members of the family of God. But they were also compelled by the Spirit of God to go out into the streets of Jerusalem, to begin meeting the needs of those in the neighborhood, expecting nothing in return because God had already given them everything they needed in Christ. Their acts of love toward others were simply a way of "paying it forward," done out of gratitude for God's amazing grace.

As a result of their visible displays of love for one another and the community, we are told they "enjoyed the favor of all the people." Who wouldn't love neighbors like this? As a result, "the Lord added to their number daily those who were being saved." Lacking a formal "evangelism program," they simply devoted themselves to being the presence of the body of Christ in their little cul-de-sac of the world. As they lived out their new mission in life, people were attracted to Jesus and wanted to have a seat at their dinner table.

In the next diagram, you can see the flywheel God first put into motion when he created the community of the church. Empowered by the Holy Spirit, people were committed together to belonging, which led them to serve, which led to the growth of the community as new people sought to belong. This Holy Spirit–empowered process is God's plan for the growth of his church.

Jesus gave his followers a vision to preach the gospel and make disciples, spreading his presence throughout the world. Beginning with the neighborhoods of Jerusalem, the relational network of the church would spread to the surrounding cities and villages of Judea, then on to the neighboring region of Samaria. From there, the vision was to see it spread to the nations — to every neighborhood in the world. By the end of Acts, this is exactly what happened. Sociologist Rodney Stark suggests from his calculations that the church grew 40 percent a year for the first three hundred years in this open-network community. This is literally a world-changing phenomenon, given that the population of the Roman Empire in AD 350 represented 56.5 percent of the entire world population![23]

And this is the kind of Christian community Bob and Karen and their two children desperately need if they want to see God's vision fulfilled in their lives.

MY STORY

Once the Johnsons begin to grasp God's story—his identity, purpose, and passions—and reconnect with what God is doing in the community of his followers, it will be time for them to discover their own individual purpose. As we've seen, most Americans *start* here: "It's all about me." But the Bible relegates this to last place. The Scriptures tell me I should begin with *God's story* and then move to *our story* before I can truly find *my story* in the world or hope to know who I really am. The "I" can only be understood in light of the "Thou."[24]

So, who am I in Christ? What is my identity in light of the story of God and the story of the church? To put it simply, I can say, "I *belong* to the body of Christ with a purpose. I have been placed within the hula hoop of God's image. I have a seat at the table. I have a purpose bigger than myself. And my sense of purpose, my unique identity, comes from being a part of God's restored community." In 1 Corinthians, Paul writes:

> Just as a body, though one, has many parts, but all its many parts form one body, so it is with Christ. For we were all baptized by one Spirit so as to form one body—whether Jews or Gentiles, slave or free—and we were all given the one Spirit to drink. Even so the body is not made up of one part but of many.
>
> Now if the foot should say, "Because I am not a hand, I do not belong to the body," it would not for that reason stop being part of the body. And if the ear should say, "Because I am not an eye, I do not belong to the body," it would not for that reason stop being part of the body. If the whole body were an eye, where would the sense of hearing be? If the whole body were an ear, where would the sense of smell be? But in fact God has placed the parts in the body, every one of them, just as he wanted them to be. If they were all one part, where would the body be? As it is, there are many parts, but one body . . .
>
> Now you are the body of Christ, and each one of you is a part of it.[25]

Rather than beginning with myself as an individual, I must

begin with an understanding that I have been included by God in the body of Christ. My identity as a Christian doesn't begin with me, my role, and my gifts, dreams, hopes, and plans. It begins with God's purposes for the church. My role is to be a *part* of that body, and God has gifted me with a unique way of being a part of his body.

So now, with my identity firmly in place as a member of the body of Christ, I can ask the question I wanted to ask at the beginning: "What is my *passion?*" What is it that drives my life each morning when I get out of bed? What captures my mind and guides my decisions as I walk through each day? What swims in my dreams when I lay my head on the pillow each night?

The answer incorporates the purpose that God has for his church: to become like Christ for the sake of others. If believers in Christ form one body and are commissioned to be the presence of Jesus on earth today, then my main commitment as an individual must be to become like Christ. In increasing measure, Christ must become more of who I am. "He must become greater; I must become less."[26]

What is God's *strategy* for us to pull this off—to become like Christ? It's simple. Like the first believers in Jerusalem, I must belong, grow, and serve.

- I must fully participate as a member of a Christian community right where I live.
- I must engage in a journey of learning to think, act, and be like Jesus.
- I must actively use my life, my gifts, and my resources to serve others.

And what do I hope all this will accomplish in the end? My hope and confidence in Christ is that I will be with God back in the new garden with the new community of those who have overturned the decision of Adam in this life through faith in Christ. Together, by God's grace, we will live forever in a new earth free from the presence of tears, hatred, disease, and death.[27]

Embedded in this biblical purpose are the first five characteristics of community. *Authority* is found in Jesus, the apostles, and their teachings. In the church are leaders—pastors and elders, as well as spiritually mature believers—who provide spiritual oversight in the lives of other believers.[28] In addition, in each family the head of the household has responsibility for assuming spiritual authority over all who occupy that household. Most often, this included servants and their families in Bible times. The spiritual development of children was not the responsibility of children's and student ministries. They didn't exist. Fathers and mothers bore the responsibility to raise and equip their children in the truth, passing along to their children what they had learned from the elders.

The community shared a *common creed* that flowed from the teachings of Scripture. Years later, the church would write and adopt memorable documents that captured this common creed in a concise way—documents such as the Apostles' and Nicene Creeds. These creeds preserve the church's oldest and most foundational beliefs, the understanding passed down from the apostles.

In addition to authority and creedal beliefs, Jesus commissioned certain *traditions* as well, including what is commonly known as Communion, or the Lord's Supper or Eucharist. As believers gathered around the table each time they met, they ate bread in remembrance of Christ's broken body. At the end of the meal, they drank from a cup of wine, remembering Christ's shed blood. This tradition, regularly practiced, kept the memory of the cross and the death of Christ central to every gathering. This tradition also invited the presence of Christ to the community each time they gathered in his name.

Standards for living were given in the letters written by Paul and several other apostles and church leaders, letters that circulated among the house churches. Virtues such as the fruit of the Spirit in Galatians 5 became normative descriptions of the type of behavior expected of Christ's followers who were yielding their lives to God.

Finally, the early followers of Jesus enjoyed a shared, *com-*

mon mission to become like Jesus and to represent his presence on earth.

What I've described here is more than just a solution to a problem, something that meets a felt need for the Johnsons and others like them caught in the trap of American individualism. This is a picture of the life and purpose God envisioned for his people before they were even born. Sadly, many who have been called by God have never tasted or seen the beauty of this vision. Why? Because our churches today are not structured and organized to live it out.

A BAD STORY

Let me explain what I mean. While individualism has been in the drinking water of the world since Genesis 3, it wasn't always the norm in the American church. Back in the 1950s and 1960s, the prosperity boom in the United States after World War II, coupled with the new superhighway system, put the pursuit of self into the fast lane. With better and faster roads—and the money to buy the automobiles to cruise on them—came the rise of intense retail competition. Instead of patronizing the "Ma and Pa" store in their own towns, people had the option of driving to the next town via the interstate for a better or cheaper product. This was the strategy Walmart employed, which allowed them to almost single-handedly strip small towns in America of their economic viability based on retail. We slowly began shifting from a loyalty to *our community* to shopping at the place that best met *our personal needs*.

What does this have to do with the American church? Well, this trend not only affected those in the retail world; it began to affect the church as well. People started driving by the local neighborhood church in their town for one that better met their needs—regardless of whether those needs were real or perceived.

When I entered full-time ministry in the 1980s, this line of thinking was mainstream. Along with other young, budding pastors, I flocked to seminars and conferences and devoured books and articles that taught me how to market my church to attract more individuals to our gatherings. The ultimate formula for growing a large church involved purchasing one hundred acres along a major interstate in a fast-growing, upper-income suburb connected to a major urban city.

The Johnson family became the target demographic. Most of the folks living in the suburbs had dug up their roots from their extended families, looking for ways to enjoy the comfort of newfound wealth and success. They came hungry to establish new friendship ties and often possessed the discretionary income to expect the best. Shopping for churches was much like shopping for cars: *find the newest and the best.*

In recent years, this pattern of consumerism has intensified. Today, it's second nature to talk about "church shopping." Many people attend several churches at different times and for different reasons, often to meet different needs. In *American Grace*, Robert Putnam from Harvard University describes a major shift in religious practice he calls "switching." Like never before in history, people switch church affiliations to meet their needs. Some, whether knowingly or unknowingly, are even switching whole religions! The largest group to which people are switching is a category Putnam calls "the Nones" — people dropping out of formal, organized religious life altogether.

Historically, the evangelical church has been the beneficiary of this switching phenomenon. Individualism and consumerism have served evangelicals well — until now. As Putnam notes:

> For most of the twentieth century ... evangelical Protestant-ism kept about three quarters of its children in the faith ... However, at least according to the General Social Survey, the retention rate of evangelical young adults plunged among the cohort who came of age at the turn of the twenty-first century, falling from 75 percent among those who came of age in the 1980s to 62 percent among those who reached adulthood in the 2000s.[29]

In other words, the growth boom in the evangelical church of the late twentieth century is now over. We are now facing a spiritual crisis as church membership declines, fueled by the individualism and consumerism of American culture.

In fear of losing members, churches now focus their attention on capturing "market share." Pastors huddle together with other pastors in different cities (that are often not their own) to share secrets on how to attract parishioners by better meeting individual needs. Here are two of the most common strategies:

- Speak to the felt needs of the individual while downplaying commitment. Six-week sermon series on relationships, marriage and family, finances, "becoming all you can be," and "living a fulfilled life" were the hot topics to attract a crowd.
- Have the best children's and student ministry program in town. One mentor told me years ago you don't have to have a world-class children's program; you just need to have one that is 10 percent better than your local competition. He knew this wasn't right, but he also knew it was what worked. It is here that parents began to slowly shift the primary responsibility for their children's spiritual development from themselves to the church.

But is this working as we hoped it would? No. Today we are living with at least two negative results of overemphasizing meeting the needs of consumerist Christians. First, many Christians are biblically illiterate. Topically based, felt-need sermons have left Christians unable to access the Bible. Instead of digging deeper for themselves, they rely on the sound bites they get from their pastors and teachers each week. George Gallup Jr. wrote this chilling conclusion from his extensive research at the end of the twentieth century:

> The churches of America face no greater challenge as we approach the next century than overcoming biblical illiteracy, and the prospects for doing so are formidable because the stark

fact is, many Christians don't know what they believe or why. Our faith is not rooted in Scripture. We revere the Bible, but we don't read it. Some observers maintain that the Bible has not in any profound way penetrated our culture.[30]

A recent study by Pew Research shows that agnostics and atheists are more religiously literate than Christians.[31] Honestly, it's hard to see how things can get much worse. When people who don't even believe that God exists know more than those who do, it's clear we have a real problem in the church.

A second problem is that children who grew up attending church are leaving the church—and they are not coming back. During my more than twenty years of service as a pastor, I've seen a large percentage of churched teens leave the nest and leave the church at the same time. But this wasn't always a cause for concern. Often, several years later, many of them would return after marrying and having kids. But recent research shows that many of those who now leave have no plans to return, even after they are married.[32]

What is the answer to this problem? I don't think the solution is for the church to intentionally become irrelevant or try to avoid meeting the needs of people. The solution is a shift away from a primary focus on meeting the needs of individual Christian consumers to becoming a spiritual community aligned to the story and purposes of God. Though it may not be immediately apparent, this vision for the church is what we as individuals truly need. People will only find their full identity as they understand and embrace the story of God and his church. And this is what Bob and Karen desperately need. It is only as we live for the sake of God, serving others in love, that we truly find a lasting sense of meaning and purpose for our lives as individuals.

Part 2

CONNECTING TO A COMMON PLACE

Chapter 6

THE PROBLEM OF ISOLATION

In a 1993 newspaper article, *Boston Globe* reporter Sally Jacobs wrote the following:

> It can never be said that Adele Gaboury's neighbors were less than responsible.
> When her front lawn grew hip-high, they had a local boy mow it down. When her pipes froze and burst, they had the water turned off. When the mail spilled out the front door, they called the police. The only thing they didn't do was check to see if she was alive.
> She wasn't.
> On Monday, police climbed her crumbling brick stoop, broke in the side door of her little blue house, and found what they believe to be the 73-year-old woman's skeletal remains sunk in a 5-foot-high pile of trash where they had apparently lain, perhaps for as long as *four* years.
> "It's not really a very friendly neighborhood," said Eileen Dugan, seventy, once a close friend of Gaboury's and whose house sits less than twenty feet from the dead woman's home. "I'm as much to blame as anyone. She was alone and needed someone to talk to, but I was working two jobs, and I was sick of her coming over at all hours. Eventually I stopped answering the door."[1]

Isolation. It's the second major obstacle to connecting in true community. This contemporary human condition flows out of the first major obstacle, namely, a culture of individualism, which promises to give us the best, only to inflict on us the disease of loneliness.

Remember the Johnson family? They struggle with isolation too, though not to the extent Adele Gaboury did. In fact, they are not even aware of their problem, for it's usually not recognized until trouble hits. But they clearly have the disease. All you have to do is reread chapter 1 to see how isolated Bob and Karen are and just how little time they have to do anything about it.

How do two highly educated, intelligent people get themselves into this place? It wasn't so much a situation they consciously chose to adopt as it was a lifestyle they were drawn into—like many of us are. Just as they were influenced by a culture of individualism, so they were influenced by a culture of isolation. As it turns out, the Johnsons were simply mimicking the lifestyles of the people they admired from a distance. Over time, they began to struggle with the same problems that had afflicted those they admired—"closet loneliness," a type of isolation that can't readily be seen in public or on social networking sites, but is nonetheless real and extraordinarily painful.

A MODERN-DAY PRISON

When did our isolation from one another become such a problem? Sociology experts point to the 1950s as the pivotal time of transition when the culture of isolation began to develop. During this era, American home designs changed, and the unique area we know today as "the suburbs" first appeared. *Fort Worth Star-Telegram* staff writer Liz Stevens explains:

> Suburbs were created after World War II to remedy a housing shortage where the land was the cheapest. The automobile made it easy for people to commute longer distances to work. The clean, spacious suburbs, as they were, fit neatly into the concept of the American Dream. What happened is that suburban developers created a housing market aimed at newly affluent populations. That, plus deteriorating inner-city ser-

vices (especially schools), racism, and other factors, catalyzed
the white middle-class's flight to the "burbs." But these devel-
opers were not architects or urban planners, and the new suburbs did not take into account basic human needs.[2]

How did suburban design work to keep our most basic needs
from being met? Consider life in a community before the 1950s.
In towns and villages built in America prior to that decade,
designers placed residences, retail stores, and workplaces within
walking distance of each other—and they did this, for the most
part, for purely practical reasons. Not everyone had an automobile, and it was far more difficult to travel from place to place. The
kind of individualized transportation we take for granted today
was not available to people, so the places they visited to meet their
needs were grouped more closely together. These densely created
communities met more than practical, physical needs. As a result
of their layout, they helped meet many of our more basic and
essential *relational* needs as well.

Paul Geisel, a professor of urban affairs at the University of
Texas at Arlington, observes:

> Before suburbs, developers would build on city streets already
> laid out for them. In a typical pre–World War II urban neigh-
> borhood, homes were built upward to promote density and
> placed close to the street. They had spacious, covered front
> porches close to the public sidewalk, making it easy to talk
> with neighbors walking back from the local market. Today's
> subdivisions feature wide, winding streets, which promote
> speedy driving. New homes with tiny front porches sit impos-
> ingly behind large private lawns. And there is no corner store,
> or public space for community gatherings.[3]

Nan Ellin, assistant professor of urban design and planning
at the University of Cincinnati, adds to Geisel's indictment by
pointing out that all the space in the suburbs is private space.[4]
People drive into their driveways, go into their houses, and never
see one another. And when television and newspapers become a

person's only source of information about his or her community, fear and isolation run rampant.

Philip Langdon, a senior editor at *Progressive Architecture* magazine, observes, "The United States has become a predominantly suburban nation, but not a very happy one ... It is no coincidence that at the moment when the United States has become a predominantly suburban nation, the country has suffered a bitter harvest of individualized trauma, family distress, and civic decay."[5] Writing for *The Atlantic Monthly*, James Howard Kunstler is intensely critical of the suburban way of life, suggesting it is "socially devastating and spiritually degrading."[6]

Architects and urban planners aren't the only ones who blame suburban life for the current angst and isolation of the American people. Communications scientist John Locke has this to say:

> The world's longest-acting vocal suppressant has undoubtedly been urbanization. After World War II, ownership of homes increased, suburbs formed, commuting intensified, and people began to isolate themselves in homes with television sets and other private amusements ... In our modern, complex societies, we are suffering from a social form of progressive aphonia. That is, we are losing our personal voices. During a period in which feelings of isolation and loneliness are on the rise, too many of us are becoming emotionally and socially mute.[7]

It's time for church leaders to take a long, hard look at the negative effects of the suburbs on the development of biblical community. The majority of churches today are located in suburban areas. And even if the church isn't in the suburbs, most of our church members live there. To meet the needs created by their isolation, many people turn to online relationships and social networking to fill the gap, yet they have little real connection to their online "friends." To develop authentic Christian community, we must carefully probe the obstacles presented each day by the places we live in. Too often, church leaders lay out biblical mandates for the church community that are good and true, and then they wonder why people just don't embrace the vision. To develop healthy community, we must not only interpret the ancient text of Scripture; we must also interpret the contemporary culture.

SOLITARY CONFINEMENT

Let's first consider the isolation that people experience in their homes. When Bob and Karen Johnson are at home, there is no one for them to talk with or connect with in a personal way. Digital connections via social media don't count — these are not face-to-face encounters. Digital technology can be very helpful, but it's only a substitute for the real thing. It cannot replace face-to-face encounters indefinitely.

When Bob and Karen are at home, they rarely see people walking by. Everyone in their neighborhood seems connected to their homestead through a closed-in automobile. Various studies have suggested that walking has decreased significantly in America in the last twenty years. John Locke proposes that many people have traded in real walking for a virtual brand: ambulating on motorized treadmills while watching television or listening to their favorite tunes, neither reaching physical destinations nor satisfying social appetites, but "pretty much keeping to themselves."[8]

Since they are not outside walking in the neighborhood, the Johnsons usually turn to television or the Internet for news. Samaritanship is seldom covered on the news (unless, of course, a young man helps an elderly woman cross the street — but the woman falls in the process and sues the man). Because sizzle is what sells, news reports tend to shape stereotyped opinions about their neighbors, leading Bob and Karen to believe that the people around them are predominantly crooks and murderers, even though a relatively few Americans are actually engaged in these crimes. Their isolation from their neighbors and the news they consume only serve to reinforce and intensify the Johnsons' fear of engaging with others. To assuage their fears, they install alarm systems, keep their doors locked at all times, and require their children to play in the backyard, which is surrounded by a six-foot-high privacy fence.

When the Johnsons go out for routine errands, they seldom encounter or relate to actual, real-life people anymore. The bank's ATM is a drive-through experience. They get their gas at a pump with no attendants. Bob swipes his credit card in an automated machine, fills up his gas tank, and takes off, not speaking to a single person in the process. He may update his Facebook status or his Twitter feed while he waits at the pump, but he doesn't engage with people in a meaningful way.

When the Johnsons travel to the large mall fifteen minutes away, they find themselves surrounded by a multitude of people, but they don't know anyone they see. People do not come to the mall to meet new people or engage in conversation with strangers. In fact, most seem to work hard at avoiding conversations.

And so, because their experiences outside the walls of their home seldom involve meaningful human interaction anyway, the Johnsons decide it's more convenient to do their shopping and banking on the Internet. While it's more convenient to do so, this practice reinforces their patterns of isolation and does nothing to help them address their underlying boredom and loneliness.

Once or twice a year, the Johnsons will venture out to the local amusement park. One year they even made the "great American Dream" journey to Disneyland. There they find themselves surrounded by thousands of people. The parks re-create the feeling of a small town and seek to give the impression that everyone you see is kinfolk or a close family friend. Yet, there's no denying the truth: the Johnsons know no one they see, and they spend much of the day standing in long lines, uncomfortably close to people they know nothing about. Happily, the theme parks have provided strategically located TV monitors to enhance the waiting experience — and help people ignore each other more comfortably. And if the monitors aren't working, they have their trusty smartphones to keep them occupied.

When the Johnsons go to work, they travel in opposite directions. When buying their house, they didn't give much thought to the location of their jobs in relation to their home. With the development of high-speed freeways initiated by President Eisenhower in the 1950s, and the fact that automobiles can now travel sixty-five or seventy miles per hour on the freeway, it didn't seem to matter that they lived far from the place where they worked. In the Johnsons' metropolitan area, the freeways have HOV (High-Occupancy Vehicle) lanes for cars with more than one person in them. On many evenings, Bob and Karen are each stuck in a freeway traffic jam on their way home, thinking about how nice it would be to hop over into an HOV lane. After all, no one else is using it!

Many evenings, the Johnsons overestimate how many errands they can run with their fast-moving metal home on wheels, with the result that they find themselves eating fast food in the car. Bob has had so many dining experiences in his car that he has even pondered buying a car equipped with a foldout dining table to go with the six preinstalled cup holders.

THE CHURCH — PART OF THE PRISON SYSTEM

As you can see, everything and everyone in the Johnsons' life is disconnected. Sadly, their church experience is no different. The Johnsons enjoy the sermons, but when they started attending the church, they had hoped to connect with others and develop a deep sense of community through involvement in a small group. Now, after a year together, they only attend one of the two monthly meetings because of their overloaded schedules. Their hearts are in the right place, but the calendars on their smartphones can't seem to make room for that meeting. So while the once-a-month gathering isn't what they would consider a "meaningful" experience, meeting every other week hasn't been any better. What they hoped would be the answer to their longing to belong has turned out to be yet another world for them to manage—one that often feels contrived and forced.

The Johnsons are thinking about checking out another church in their area. They can't pinpoint exactly what is wrong with the church they're in, but they know their needs simply aren't being met. So, like most Americans, they think about moving on to something new. It's likely that over the next year or so, the Johnsons will slip out the door of the church, unnoticed, never to return. Someone may call them to check in, or they may run into a well-meaning church member who will ask where they've been, but for the most part, their absence will go unnoticed.

Does this sound like your church?

Chapter 7

CHARACTERISTICS OF A COMMON PLACE

A line from the 1993 box-office-hit movie *Jurassic Park* aptly describes the American lifestyle. At one point in the movie, a group of people made up of a lawyer and some "salt of the earth" paleontologists are sitting around a large conference table. It finally sinks in that eccentric billionaire John Hammond has created a genetic wonder world of prehistoric dinosaurs reconstructed from the DNA of dinosaur blood extracted from ancient mosquitoes. The paleontologists are caught up in the marvel of actually seeing flesh on the bones they have been digging up for years; the lawyer sees dollar signs. Only one character (Dr. Ian Malcolm, played by Jeff Goldblum) offers a stern word of caution and concern. He says, "Your scientists were so preoccupied with whether or not they could, they didn't stop to think if they *should*!"[1]

This is equally true when we apply it to the American way of life that has developed and become the cultural norm over the past sixty years. As Americans built their sprawling suburbs, superhighway systems, and faster automobiles, the only question being asked was, "Can we do it?" — not "Should we do it?" As with most scientific discoveries and technological developments, a key issue is not *if* we can do something but the *impact* it will have on our way of life. And unforeseen consequences resulted from these decisions.

We ignored what our ancestors had done in designing places

where people can live together and grow in community, and we chose the path of convenience and personal comfort. We ignored traditional principles of design that lead to flourishing community life and created a system that promotes isolation, catering to our individual tastes. While modern-day circumstances are certainly different, Americans have essentially rejected the wisdom of the past, much like the people of Israel did when they received this charge from Jeremiah over twenty-five hundred years ago:

> This is what the LORD says:
>
> "Stand at the crossroads and look;
>   ask for the ancient paths,
> ask where the good way is, and walk in it,
>   and you will find rest for your souls.
> *But you said, 'We will not walk in it.'*"[2]

Many of us, like Bob and Karen Johnson, have made decisions about the places and spaces we inhabit day to day, and they directly affect our ability to grow and thrive in community with others. In this chapter, we will see that healthy community is dependent on location, space, and context, and we'll examine five characteristics of a healthy community united around a common place.

FIVE CHARACTERISTICS OF COMMUNITY AROUND A COMMON PLACE

When Americans were building their suburban homes and cities at the close of the twentieth century, they not only ignored the lessons of the past; they ignored what the Bible teaches about *biblical* community. Biblical community is a way of referring to a collection of people gathered around a common biblical purpose and common principles. We should realize that a group of people can be committed to the Bible from its opening to its conclusion and still not be a community. By the same token, a group of people can experience community together and not be biblical in its purpose. Biblical community is formed when purpose and principles unite to create the foundation for the community and its life together.

But several other factors influence how the community is experienced. In fact, five common characteristics are shared by groups of people who experience true community *around a common place*. When these characteristics are fully functioning, they facilitate the chemistry needed for good community life. When one or more of these characteristics is absent, we intuitively sense that something essential has been lost. If all five qualities are missing in the life of a community, it's likely the group is not experiencing biblical community, regardless of their commitment to the Bible, its purposes, and its principles. As you read about each characteristic, evaluate whether it is present and functioning within your "community."

Spontaneity

Spontaneity is defined in the dictionary as "acting or taking place without any outside force or cause." Places of effective community exhibit this characteristic. While some gatherings are planned with rich tradition and elaborate ritual, most of the gatherings in a community are unplanned — that is, spontaneous.

Take, for example, the small-town neighborhoods in America before the 1950s. People typically had only one car per family, and many people simply used public transportation. If a family did own a car, it was usually driven to work by the man of the house. Throughout the course of the week, the wife needed to shop for groceries or other staple items; she may even have needed to get to the town square's post office to check for mail. And everyone else in the neighborhood needed to do the same. Houses were located within walking distance of the places where people worked and the retail shops where people purchased what they needed. As a result, several times each day, people in the neighborhood would walk by other homes — homes built close to the street, with a sidewalk between the house and the street. Except for the coldest winter days, family members were often outside, sitting on the front porch and sipping iced tea or coffee. They would spend time outside because there was no central air-conditioning in the house and the porch was shaded and designed to catch the breeze. There was usually nothing of particular interest on television—even if the family owned one. Whenever Mrs. Jones would walk by on her way to the grocery store for some fresh eggs or flour, the family on the porch would call out a greeting. They might even take the time to "shoot the breeze." These interactions weren't planned events; they were spontaneous encounters in which human contact was made and conversation was shared.

Consider the lives of the children in these neighborhoods. While Dad was at work, did Johnny play at Billy's house on the other side of town? Did Mom pull her seven-passenger van out of the garage and take her beloved son over to Billy's house twenty minutes away? Of course not. Children were expected to play with the other kids in the neighborhood, associating with the children who lived near them. There were relatively few organized sports. Parents did more than chauffeur and entertain. Children were expected to use their imaginations and, on a nonexistent monetary budget, create a day filled with spontaneous play. There was accountability to others since other neighbors were watching or working in their backyards, which were open, not protected by six-foot-high privacy fences. If little Johnny was doing something he shouldn't be doing, Mom and Dad would likely know about it before he sat down at the supper table.

Lest you assume I am romanticizing the 1950s, I want to make it clear that this kind of spontaneous activity is simply an example of a way of life that had existed for centuries. Though it has varied from culture to culture and has changed in various ways over time, the most common ways people experienced community with others were based around a common place—a geographic context they shared in common with one another. Only in the last sixty years have people been robbed of the spontaneity afforded by a shared space.

Jesus experienced this type of community with his disciples.

The disciples didn't have to schedule teaching times or mealtimes with Jesus, because they were always together. The Old Testament patriarch Jacob didn't have to wonder whether his oldest son, Reuben, would remember to call each night, because Reuben was living in the tent next door. Every night the family members would gather by the fire and tell stories and laugh together. For their entertainment, they didn't travel twenty minutes to the late-night movie theater, equipped with the latest high-tech features, stadium seating, and a football-field-size screen. When the sun went down, the lights went out. Only the light from the oil lamp or a small fire was available for family members who wished to stay awake and talk.

We have lost the opportunity for spontaneity that naturally existed when communities were based around a common place, and, as John Locke has said, "Our spontaneity has taken a plunge."[3] Most Americans don't even know they have lost something essential, but there is an undeniable longing for it.

In the last decade of the twentieth century, two of the most popular television shows, *Seinfeld* and *Friends*, consistently received the top awards from the People's Choice Awards, whose honorees are chosen by a special opinion poll of thousands of Americans. Though the shows were different in many ways, they had in common a small group of friends who regularly gathered in a common place. In both shows, the characters spent significant time in one another's apartments, often stopping by spontaneously more times in a half hour than most "real" Americans would ever do with their friends in a year. *Seinfeld* promoted itself as a show "about nothing," but it certainly wasn't about nothing; it was about a group of friends spontaneously spending time together, talking about everyday stuff and loving every minute of it. Whether they realized it or not, the people watching the show longed for that kind of spontaneous, close-knit community as well.

To find fulfillment in their search to belong, people need a small band of friends who spontaneously come in and out of each other's lives. Randomly commenting on blogs and online status updates isn't enough. The small group the Johnsons joined at their church seemed to hold promise initially, but the result was never achieved. Small group interactions tend to be planned events with a clear agenda, leaving little room for spontaneity. Work schedules, child care demands, and busy lives often require that the details of the next meeting are planned out before the current one ends. To be clear, it's not that the Johnsons and the other group members don't want spontaneous encounters; *it simply isn't the way their lives work.* The geographic and physical distance between them can only be overcome through careful planning and a commute. There are simply no places for them to meet where spontaneity can be experienced. The characteristics that lead to healthy community tend to rub against the grain of our contemporary culture, but this shouldn't surprise us. The "me" world we've created for ourselves is not compatible with the principles that govern biblical community.

Availability

The characteristic of availability is akin to spontaneity. Those who have found a meaningful experience of life together discover that most of the time it happens when their comrades are ready, willing, and eager to lend an ear or a hand — or even to offer the simple gift of their presence. It's not that these people do not have important things to do; it's just that they see being available to each other as more important than most of the things we in today's society deem important.

There was a time when "screen" was commonly understood to be a lightweight, meshed-wire door designed to let fresh air in the house and keep bugs out. But when a more solid, inner door was left open, the screen door was also a signal to the neighbors that someone was home and that others were invited to stop in for a visit. In our suburban way of life, however, "screen" now means something else entirely.

We set up screens around our lives, not to signal availability, but to keep people away, like screen doors that keep bugs out. Our solid, inner doors are tightly closed and locked. Peepholes, caller ID, e-mail filters, and voice mail give us the option to say yes to those we want to speak with and no to others. And this is not all bad, certainly. To survive in the digital world, we must learn to adapt and protect our time and our ability to focus on what is most important. Today's technologies have made us immediately accessible to everyone on the planet through phone calls, e-mails, and texts. For some, the majority of the calls and e-mails they receive are from strangers trying to sell them something. Still, though they understand when people don't visit or call because everybody is really so very busy today, they long for a visit or call from *someone who cares.*

In the past, if a person wanted to chat with a friend, the chances were good that the friend would be available. Why? Because they lived within walking distance of one another. Close proximity to one another and lack of mobility meant people were more available. People were more available because there were fewer options, fewer alternative places for them to visit.

As we saw earlier, it's a sad truth that most of us don't know the people who live around us. Instead of getting to know our neighbors, those who live closest to us, we typically engage in *contractual friendships* with people who share an affinity or a common interest. No longer are people primarily united by geographic proximity. We spend time with those we like best, regardless of where they happen to live. Why? Because we can. In contractual friendships we try to "associate up" — usually spending time with those in the same or slightly higher social class. But there are significant problems in adopting this form of contrived community.

First and foremost, associating only with those we like isn't pleasing to God. Jesus scolded the religious leaders of his day for trying to define one's neighbor in this self-centered way. One expert of the law tried to justify himself as a good neighbor, but he wanted his evaluation to include only those of his own race and status. In response, Jesus told the famous parable of the good

Samaritan, showing that this lawyer's understanding of community was flawed, influenced by his own prejudices and selfish interests and not by the purposes of God.[4]

In an article in the *Cornell Law Review*, Greg Alexander challenges this new basis on which friendships are formed. Alexander sees many of the tensions we have in our relationships as a basic conflict between contractarian and communitarian theories of community. The contractarian theory of community views individuals as atomistic entities, not connected to each other except as they agree to be connected for personal benefit. In contrast, the communitarian ideal sees "individuals ... embedded in society, connected not only through their common humanity but through the social structures they jointly create and benefit from."[5] In other words, the contractarian view prioritizes the individual, seeing community as a collection of individuals coming together for mutual benefit. The communitarian view tends to focus on society, seeing the identity of individuals primarily in relationship to the structures they belong to in society.

A significant problem with contractual friendships is that they limit availability. As time and practice have proved, when our focus is on our own individual pursuits, we tend to not be as available for one other. Time together requires precise planning. We may have an immediate need, but we aren't likely to drive across town on the hunch that a friend will be home and free to talk. We might try to call or connect online with a friend, but these types of connections, though they can be helpful substitutes, are still a step removed from a real-life connection with another human being. The computer screen is a glowing wall between people that inhibits true depth of community. Intentions may be good, but they don't really meet our needs and fulfill our desires.

Picture a monk who is unhappy with the people who reside in his monastery. Because he doesn't like the people he sees each day, he decides to develop his deepest friendships with several guys in a monastery thirty miles away. "Ludicrous," you say. "It would never happen." And you'd be right. Monks lack mobility, but they are able to maintain the highest level of availability to one another because they share a common place. This is one of the reasons their experience of community is such a positive one. I have a hunch that if we hired a Benedictine monk to guide us toward a simple way of life, he would tell us we can't get where we want to go, given the lifestyle we have chosen. He would likely recommend a "radical reinventing" that includes freeing up more time to be available for others (and perhaps shutting off our phones more often).

The question behind the solution is clear: How badly do we want community? Are we willing to sacrifice our existing lifestyle to experience something new?

Frequency

Another characteristic of community that promotes the value of a common place is frequency. Simply put, people who are satisfied with the experience of community are spontaneous and available, and they also spend a great deal of time together. In the book of Acts, we are given a rare peek into the wonderful and effective community of the "First Church of Jerusalem": "They devoted themselves to the apostles' teaching and to the fellowship, to the breaking of bread and to prayer."[6]

Luke tells us that this close-knit group of Christ followers devoted themselves to four principal things: the apostles' teaching, fellowship, breaking bread, and prayer. Beginning in Acts 2:43 and continuing for several verses, we are shown the outcome of their community devotion. Miracles took place, people's lives were changed, the believers cared deeply and sacrificially for each other, and new people came to know Christ—and as a result their group grew rapidly. The Bible says they even enjoyed a spectacular reputation in the surrounding community.

But there is one additional aspect of their fellowship most modern-day believers overlook. How often did they gather? Luke tells us plainly in Acts 2:46: "Every day they continued to meet together."

One of the big issues in Bob and Karen's church is *how often* a small group should meet. Should they meet once a week, every other week, or just once a month? Studies of healthy community life tell us that neither once a week nor every other week is enough to create real community. If we want an outcome similar to that experienced in the "First Church of Jerusalem," we must be willing to put in the same level of commitment they did. It doesn't make sense to input one-seventh or one-fourteenth of all our available time and expect 100 percent of their results.

You are no doubt shaking your head in disbelief at such a suggestion. How realistic is it for believers to interact with one another every day? But before you dismiss this as crazy or unrealistic, remember that *this kind of daily interaction has been a dominant characteristic and requirement of community throughout history.* And it can be today as well.

For example, if you viewed video footage of a small group of Christians in a village in India who gather every day to pray, you would see the depth of their love for each other because it's that evident. Christians in India need our financial resources to help them accomplish Christ's mission, but they don't necessarily need our style of church. In fact, one of the worst things we can do is to try to "colonialize" the American church model in India, imposing our structures and cultural priorities on them. Instead, we should rejoice in what God is doing in their midst, provide financial resources when needed, and willingly invite them to teach us how to be a biblical Christian community. There may be a few things we can stand to learn in this area!

Even in a place like a college fraternity house, multiple encounters in a given day with the same people are fairly normal. In part, this may explain why so many people have such fond memories of their college days and often look back on that time as a positive experience of community. When you add to that experience a common commitment to Christ (like the ministry of Campus Crusade for Christ or InterVarsity), you can see why the community life of a Christian attending college tends to damage that graduate's chances of a happy assimilation into today's typical "individualized" church. We need to recognize that our American lifestyle does not represent the norm in the world today—it's the exception. The world we've created for ourselves in twenty-first-century American culture pulls us apart from this type of daily interaction with others, making us some of the loneliest people in the world.

This social condition has progressively worsened over the past sixty years, but the effect has been subtle. Like the frog placed in a pot of room-temperature water is oblivious to the water temperature's slow rise, few of us realize we are almost at a boiling point. Again, John Locke lays bare the truth in his revealing study of American life:

> Each year in a large and respected poll, the General Social Survey, Americans from a range of demographic groups are asked how often they spend an evening socializing with a neighbor. In 1974 nearly one in four Americans visited with a neighbor several times a week. By 1994 that figure had declined to 16 percent. But in 1994 there was a shocking increase in the number of people who had never spent an evening with a neighbor—from one in five to nearly one in three—a 41 percent increase since the same question was asked twenty years earlier.[7]

The isolated places in which we live have given rise to an unprecedented need for practicing counselors. Certainly, some of the need for these mental health professionals is justified by the fact that we all face struggles over the course of our lives. Some people today, however, employ the counselor as a "paid friend." I cautiously suggest that roughly 80 percent of this industry has been created as an alternative to the community that has been lost to us as a culture. I see churches struggling to create new forms of community, trying to establish strong, properly functioning small groups in a time when "friendships" are being outsourced to paid professionals. People pay someone to share their struggles, but never reveal what is going on in their lives to the people in their small group—their "biblical" community.

As leaders strategize to find new and creative ways to develop community life in the church, they must also find ways to address these issues. Fundamental to this is the need to recognize the power of frequency. As Jim Petersen has said, "Body Life is 24 hours a day, 7 days a week, and embraces the full spectrum of our activities."[8] If people are not willing to restructure their lives and their time to meet more regularly together, the experience of true community will continue to elude them. Unless we make the necessary changes, we will never have the kind of community the "First Church of Jerusalem" had. If we aren't willing to change, we should stop pretending it's possible.

Sharing Meals

You may be surprised to find something as mundane as sharing a meal on this list of the top characteristics of community, but I don't apologize for including it. Note carefully, however, that this is about more than eating—it's about *eating together*. Writer Jeffrey Weiss of the *Dallas Morning News* tells a story about Dr. Daniel Sack, author of *Whitebread Protestants: Food and Religion in American Culture*. He begins his article with these words: "The casseroles and Jell-O molds of the traditional Protestant potluck supper may seem unlikely sources for serious insight. But Daniel Sack, associate director for the Material History of American Religion Project, says there is important information about belief and custom hidden among the beanie-weenies."[9] Food may seem incidental to community, but it plays a more significant role than many assume.

It's easy to miss this when we read and study the Bible, but when we pay attention to it we immediately notice that eating together was a significant part of life in both the Old and New Testaments. We also see its importance in the early church experience: "Every day they continued to meet together … They broke bread in their homes and ate together with glad and sincere hearts."[10] There is something vitally important and special about sharing a meal together. Just consider the fact that the Lord's Supper (an act of the partaking of food and drink together) is one of the few New Testament rituals we are commanded to observe. Eberhard Arnold, who founded the Bruderhof Communities, put it eloquently: "Symbolism can be found in the trivialities of existence, too: when approached with reverence, even daily rites such as mealtime can become consecrated festivals of community."[11]

The concept of regularly eating together is now somewhat foreign to our American culture. It has become increasingly rare for the average American family to share more than two or three meals together during the week.[12] Looking more closely at the Johnson family, you will notice that children's sports activities and extra hours spent working late at the office account for most of their missed meals. Try suggesting to your friends that you start sharing a meal together a couple of times a week, and see how many of them laugh at you. Most of us can't imagine doing such a thing because we already feel overwhelmed by the goal of having mealtimes with our immediate families.

Again, I'll be the first to admit that given our current lifestyles, this *is* an unreasonable expectation — which is precisely why any progress we want to make toward real community will take a major lifestyle restructuring. To recapture the depth and power of biblical community, we must be willing to practice eating together. We need to make room for opportunities to regularly share meals with others.

Geography

Underlying each of the previous four characteristics is the idea of geography and shared context — a common place. The simple truth is that effective communities are found where people live in close proximity to each other — and the closer the better! Consider Jesus and his disciples. To those he encountered, Jesus extended the invitation, "Come, follow me," not "Come, make the commute each day." The late Henri Nouwen left a prestigious

Ivy League professorship to become the executive director of L'Arche, a residential community for mentally and physically challenged people. He did so because he perceived this to be a divine call on his life. What he found at L'Arche was the richest community he had ever experienced. Soon after his arrival, however, he fell apart and had an emotional breakdown.[13] Christian psychologist Larry Crabb offers this insightful commentary regarding Nouwen's experience:

> When he gave them [his prestigious career and all it offered him] up for life with people who were not impressed by such things, perhaps his repressed desire to be loved rather than merely admired overwhelmed him. The taste of love that his new community provided may have awakened deeper longings than he ever knew existed, longings that he feared would never be satisfied.[14]

Why do I mention Henri Nouwen's experience? Because it reminds us that community does not necessarily require profound intelligence or common interest to experience its power. It may simply require being geographically close—close enough to be available for each other spontaneously and frequently enough to feel safe and loved.

One woman wrote of her experience of living with a group of five other women in one house. While not everything about the experience was positive, on the whole it was a remarkably meaningful time for her. After getting married, however, she could no longer be involved in this type of residential community with other women. Instead, she sought community by attending her new husband's church-sponsored small group. Consider her honest assessment of that experience: "Living in residential community raised my standards. For several months I attended my husband's church small group. I thought, 'This is intimacy? This is challenge?' After years of prayer, fellowship, and everyday life with five close roommates, a weekly meeting with a dozen people seemed shallow."[15]

As I've said before, my intent is not to knock small group ministry. When we look at the Johnsons' suburban small group experience, it's not a *bad* thing; it's just not enough to meet their innate longing for community. For their experience to go to the next level of meaning, it should be "pedestrian accessible." My point is that the Johnsons will need to seek out relationships with those who live closest to them. They can form contract friendships with a collection of the brightest, smartest, strongest, prettiest, and most spiritual people in their community to form a small group, but if they are not in relationships based on close proximity (that is, living within walking distance), they will still feel as though something is missing.

Of course, many people raise objections to this notion of geographic-based relationships. With online social networking it is possible to have and maintain friendships with anyone, at anytime, and anywhere in the world for a minimal cost. Critics may also say that social networking has shown that friendships do not rely on geography—and they would be right. I'm not objecting to online relationships, nor am I suggesting that such relationships lack value. I am simply suggesting that to overcome the persistent loneliness we experience in our lives, we need to rediscover the value of relating to others in our local neighborhoods. We naturally want to defend the quality of the relationships we have already formed, and we may find challenges in forming relationships with those in our neighborhoods. Still, I ask you to keep an open mind and consider that something may be missing in your life, something that can only be filled by developing relationships with those who live near you.

Geographic-based community has its fair share of problems and challenges. Just ponder for a moment the small, old-fashioned town with a main street—a town where everyone works and shops and houses are all pretty much within walking distance of each other. Some who lived there would be the first to say they do not experience intimacy in that environment, that they feel nothing but an invasion of their privacy! Shared knowledge of the happenings in your local neighborhood can be both positive and negative. Some use such knowledge to feed the local gossip mill. Yet we should keep in mind that this isn't true community; it's "community without character." Healthy communities will develop ways of addressing such problems through discipline, accountability, and loving confrontation. It's still better to have a community with challenges but with potential for growth and change than to have no community at all.

Consider the alternative. Most people who live in suburban America lead fairly private lives. News about their life is kept secret (at least in part because people don't care). They gain privacy, but only at the cost of real community with those around them. Take a man and a woman with three children and stick them together under one roof, and you'll get moments of intense conflict and irritation. But most people will not want to up and leave, forsaking their family just because their relationships have challenging moments. They choose to stick with these relationships, not because they are easy, but because they give meaning to life and shape their identity. So it is with Christian community as well. When people are spread out geographically, they typically only see each other once or twice a week at most. For some, this level of interaction is appealing to the schedule, but it is unlikely that meaningful relationships will form from these interactions (though there are always exceptions). One of the biggest challenges leaders face in seeking to build community is convincing people to choose what may not be easy but is nonetheless good for their personal and spiritual growth.

Close geographic proximity has a profound impact on the health of a community because it enables and empowers many of the other place-dependent characteristics of community. As we have seen, close proximity provides opportunities for spontaneity. It offers simple accessibility, which means people are more likely to be available to others. It provides opportunities for more frequent meetings and makes sharing meals easier in the face of busy schedules. The plain truth is that if Bob and Karen were to find their most significant relationships within their neighbor-hood, these relationships would inevitably begin to meet some of their deepest needs. Because the Johnsons are a product of their individualized American culture, they cannot see how any of this could work for them.

It's wrong, however, to dismiss an idea because our current circumstances seem to make its realization impossible. To make the impossible a reality, we'll need to overcome the fears and doubts associated with this new way of living. People will need to taste the potential for something new. They will need to embrace beliefs that activate and empower a commitment to a new way of relating to others. And it will feel awkward at first. In the next chapter, we'll look at the core beliefs needed to pursue this brand of community, even when it rubs against the grain of the culture.

Chapter 8

REDISCOVERING NEIGHBORHOOD

When Bob and Karen Johnson begin to think about simplifying the many disconnected worlds they manage, they sense a spark of hope that they may find some relief from their current situation. Maybe they can finally get to the heart of what really matters in life and find time to slow down to spend more time with their family and with those around them. But almost immediately following this sigh of relief comes a gasp of confusion and doubt: "How can we pull this off? Where do we even start?" Excitement quickly gives way to fear. Most people stop right there. They are paralyzed by their circumstances and the hard work of change, and they give up.

Let's be honest. Change is hard. Breaking habits isn't easy. We read in the Bible that Israel wanted to return to a miserable life of slavery in Egypt because the journey they had to make through the desert to the Promised Land seemed too difficult for them. It's not that they enjoyed their slavery; they just knew how to cope with it better than the uncertainties awaiting them in the desert journey. This same temptation faces the Johnsons—and many of us today. We need to remember that what currently defines our lifestyle is just not working for us, as comfortable as it may be. Something new must be attempted, because if we continue to use the same methods, we will be guaranteed the same results. Francis Bacon once wrote, "He that will not apply new remedies must expect new evils."[1] In other words, the status quo that is sucking the life out of you right now will continue sucking the life out of you. One year from now, five years from now, your situation will only be worse. The time to act is now.

Long-lasting behavior change is rooted in deeply held beliefs. The Johnsons need to be convinced in their minds that although the journey may be long and difficult, it is the right and best path for their feet to tread. Here are some big ideas for them to consider that can keep them committed to the task of creating lasting community.

THEOLOGY OF PLACE

The Bible teaches that God is spirit, that he doesn't occupy space or time. Yet we should consider what God did when he created the world. In the beginning, God created a *place* in the midst of the cosmos we call earth. On this planet, he created another *place*, a garden, where he made a man and a woman with physical bodies. We know angelic spirits were already in existence, but God chose to make human beings with the stuff of the earth — physical matter. Then he chose to meet with the man and woman he had made. He walked with them in a *place*, in the garden in the cool of the day.[2] God's actions in these passages in Genesis communicate much, but at least one thing is evident in what God did: place matters.

Consider God's relationship with the people of Israel. God promises to Abraham in Genesis 12 and 15 that he will give the descendants of Abraham land of their own. As the story unfolds, we see it takes over six hundred years for the promise of the land to be fulfilled, but God is faithful. Why a promise of land? Because physical space matters. Land is more than somewhere to live; it represents the context for relationship, communicates security, and informs the people's understanding of God and what life is like under the reign and rule of God.

When Judah was in the process of returning to Jerusalem after seventy years of captivity under God's hand of discipline, this is how Zechariah described the life they were returning to enjoy: "This is what the LORD Almighty says: 'Once again men and women of ripe old age will sit in the streets of Jerusalem, each of them with cane in hand because of their age. The city streets will be filled with boys and girls playing there.' "[3]

God's promise of land for his people was about more than just the dirt and trees. It was a promise of life together, a *place* to call home. It was a promise of neighborhood life and block parties. In his promise to Israel, God connected their life as a community with the place he provided for them.

But this idea isn't found only in the Old Testament. Consider Jesus, who came down into our space and took on flesh.[4] Eugene Peterson puts it this way in *The Message*: "The Word [Jesus] became flesh and blood, and moved into the neighborhood."[5] Isaiah tells us one of Jesus' names is "Immanuel," which literally means, "God with us."[6] God could have communicated with us through divine e-mails, texts, and tweets, but he chose instead to go through the hassle of actually coming down to be with us, face-to-face in the flesh. Jesus spent time with people. He touched them, and they were healed. He saw their wounds and wiped their tears. He laughed with them around the evening campfire. He ate with them around the dinner table. He was present and accounted for in his relationships.

And when we read about the resurrection, we learn that when Jesus died and rose again, he did so not as a spiritual being, divorced from the material world. No, he rose again with a real, physical body. The tomb was empty—his physical body gone.[7] It was not replaced or discarded—it was resurrected. The disciples touched him where the nails had been driven into his hands.[8] Jesus showed himself to over five hundred people before ascending into the heavens to be seated at the right hand of the Father.[9] This teaches us that God values the world he has made. He values the people he has created. He values the places he has designed.

Consider how the story of God concludes. Revelation 21 and 22, the last two chapters of the Bible, tell a story much like the first two chapters of the Bible. In the end, the place God made "in the beginning" is not utterly destroyed or abandoned; it is renewed. We read the promise of a new, physical earth, a newly constructed city, and we hear the good news that God is once again coming down to be with us in a place we know—this world we live in, renewed and healed.

> Then I saw "a new heaven and a new earth," for the first heaven and the first earth had passed away, and there was no longer any sea. I saw the Holy City, the new Jerusalem, coming down out of heaven from God, prepared as a bride beautifully dressed for her husband. And I heard a loud voice from the throne saying, "Look! God's dwelling place is now among the people, and he will dwell with them. They will be his people, and God himself will be with them and be their God."[10]

When Jesus communicates the promise of heaven coming to earth, he tells us he is creating actual places, real homes that will be placed in a new city, the new Jerusalem. Talk about an extreme home makeover! Just like in the TV show where they meet someone's needs by building a house if a mere renovation of their home won't cut it, our host, Jesus, will announce that it's time to "move that bus" away from the front of an actual home to reveal a real place in a new neighborhood in the city of Jerusalem. We, too, will experience a bodily resurrection and receive new bodies not subject to death, disease, or decay, and we will sit on the front porches of our new eternal pad that is paid for in full with the blood of Christ.[11]

We don't know if there will be social networking in the new earth. We may not use phones or have e-mail. But one thing is certain: there will be neighborhoods—real places where we live, meet, and relate in community with other people.

SOCIOLOGY OF PLACE

In researching the American quest for community, Princeton professor Robert Wuthnow writes:

I used to be in this group of people who met weekly, and that was a specific circle of friends where we really did help each other out, sharing problems, sharing whatever. Now my friends are more linear. I'm friends with this person and I'm friends with that person, but I don't have a circle of friends who sort of know each other right now.[12]

Wuthnow's comments illuminate the reason those of us who live like the Johnsons must seek a new paradigm for living and relating to others.

The difference is that a circle provides for more internal accountability than a series of linear relationships. If your friends don't know each other, you (even without thinking about it) play up one side of yourself to this friend and a different side to someone else. One friend, for example, can be a confidant on spiritual issues; another can share babysitting but have no spiritual points of intersection at all. When your friends all know each other because they are in the same group, you are more likely to experience the tendency toward personal consistency that fellow believers refer to as discipleship. Your friends can compare notes to see if you are treating them all the same. They can decide whether you need advice. For them to all get along with each other, they are likely to agree on certain principles themselves. And this agreement will minimize your chances of being pulled in widely different directions.[13]

Bob and Karen long to have a circle of friends with whom they can mutually share their dreams and fears. But a series of disconnected linear relationships will never achieve what they want; it will take a cohesive *circle* of friends. If the Johnsons are serious about experiencing biblical community, they must begin by exchanging their current linear strategy for a circular one. Some will argue that there are many ways to get what they want, but experience and history have proved that people who *share a common place* are in the best position to achieve what the Johnsons are seeking. Sharing geographic space—a neighborhood, an apartment building, a college dormitory, a military barracks—

facilitates the four characteristics of community laid out in the last chapter: spontaneity, availability, frequency, and sharing meals.

PHYSIOLOGY OF PLACE

We have a wonderful nonprofit organization called Threads of Love housed in a building on our church property. Their mission? To make special clothing for the many premature babies born in San Antonio each week. They also provide the smallest of clothes, more like little pockets, for stillborn babies to wear for their brief time of being held by Mom and Dad and then to wear for their burial. These threads of love provide immense dignity for both the little baby and the parents. I smile and cry every time I visit this building filled with mostly elderly women pouring the love of Christ out of their thimble-protected fingers. They knit wardrobes of grace.

I'll never forget my first visit. Joe, the eighty-two-year-old volunteer director of the ministry, was giving the tour. When we got to the far left side of the building, Joe held up a small, soft blanket and said, "This is one of our most popular items. It's called a kangaroo blanket." He paused and waited for me to ask the obvious: "What is a kangaroo blanket?" His answer left me shaking my head in amazement.

Kangaroos give birth to underdeveloped young called joeys. The young are placed in the mother kangaroo's famous pouch, leaving the infant to spend hours a day "skin to skin" with her and yet kept warm by the outer blanket of fur. Undeveloped countries that lack the resources to provide incubators for preterm babies tried this method with amazing success. The naked preemie is laid on the bare chest of the mother for hours at a time. Today, it is estimated that 82 percent of neonatal intensive care units in the United States use kangaroo care. The kangaroo blanket, sewn with love, serves as a modesty blanket and creates a connection of intimacy for the mother and baby, much like the furry pouch of the kangaroo.

Research shows that this form of care has many benefits to the baby: normalized heart, temperature, and respiratory rates; increased weight gain; fewer infections; reduced risk of respiratory tract disease; improved cognitive development; decreased stress levels; reduced pain responses; normalized growth; positive motor development; improved sleep patterns; colic intervention; and an earlier discharge from the hospital.[14] This is just one of many scientific and medical studies that remind us we cannot neglect or avoid our need for physical connection with real people. We must acknowledge the "physiology of place"—that we were created for face-to-face, skin-to-skin, eyeball-to-eyeball, hand-shaking, neck-hugging community.

EVEN OPRAH THINKS IT'S A GOOD IDEA

Oprah Winfrey once aired an episode in which she discussed research conducted by *The British Medical Journal*. The research demonstrated that happiness spreads from person to person up to three connections away. "If your friend's friend's friend becomes happier, it ripples through the network and affects you," says a medical sociology professor at Harvard Medical School, Dr. Nicholas Christakis.[15] The study revealed that *proximity* plays an important part in the spread of happiness. A happy sibling who is a mile away can increase your probability of happiness by up to 14 percent; a nearby friend, by 25 percent; and a next-door neighbor, by 34 percent! Oprah concluded the show by suggesting that one of the best ways to increase your happiness is getting to know two of your neighbors.

A RADICAL REINVENTING

I realize it is not reasonable to expect that everyone will move from the suburbs to a small town. So, given the scenario of people remaining in a suburban or urban context, how can a family like the Johnsons begin to create community? Because of the architectural forces that work against achieving community in the suburbs, their pursuit will have to be intentional. It will require making difficult changes and learning the art of saying no to a vast array of opportunities available to them. It will be a process that struggles to coexist with the transitioning of lifestyle paradigms. If you venture on this journey, you will be pioneering an ancient idea for a new day—and pioneers are always criticized and misunderstood. If you deeply embrace the belief that place matters, and if you have the stamina to stick with it and follow the governing principles as purely as you know how, you will one day begin to realize dividends from your investment. It may take six months, or two years, or more.

Let me share several specific tips for engineering your "great escape." If you have a tough time seeing how this vision can be accomplished in your current neighborhood, view these steps as though you are going to move to a new place and make a fresh start. One of the biggest mistakes people make today is looking only to buy a house, not to find a neighborhood. We spend a lot of money for an inspection to ensure the quality of the home's construction, yet because relationships are more important than sticks and bricks, common sense suggests it would be wise to conduct a neighborhood inspection as well. Even if you are not planning a move, seeing your current neighborhood through the eyes of an outsider can bring fresh vision to your work.

Cut Down the Commute

If at all possible, live in the neighborhood closest to your workplace. If it isn't possible, try to rearrange your schedule to avoid traffic jams. If you're spending two or three hours a day commuting, it will be difficult to have much time left for anything else. With the improvements and efficiencies of technology, more and more people are able to work remotely, which usually means working out of your home or at the local Starbucks. While this isn't possible for everyone, it may be something you decide to pursue with your employer. Some studies have shown that productivity goes up dramatically for those who work away from the office, and you may remember that Bob and Karen Johnson both did some work in the evenings when they had trouble getting their work done at the office during the day.

Live Off a Single Income

If you have younger children, it may make sense to have one person at home full-time to manage meals and oversee the children's homework so they get it done early enough to leave time open in the evening. If you begin these tasks after daytime work hours, they eat into those precious evening hours for experiencing daily community with others. For many suburban families where both the mother and father work and perhaps commute long distances, it is virtually impossible to have meals together as a family, let alone to eat meals with neighbors. (Incidentally, for the single parent, how beneficial it would be if at least a few meals a week could be shared with neighbors to lighten his or her load.)

If this solution is not within your grasp, two other options may be considered: First, as I've already suggested, take advantage of today's technology and pursue work that can be done at home with flexible work hours. The second idea is simple but a bit more radical. Look for a home that can be funded on a reduced amount of income, preferably on only one income. The irony of American family economics is that we purchase big and beautiful homes that take two incomes to sustain, and yet we don't spend much time in them!

Choose Stability

The United States population is characterized by high mobility.[16] This means that we move around a lot. The most common reason is a company transfer or a new job. Now it is certainly true that on occasion work will dry up in a town or city, forcing one to move on to provide the basic necessities for the family. The reality, more often than not, however, is that people move to chase perhaps an extra $5,000 to $10,000 a year.

The difficulty with this mind-set is that it doesn't provide an opportunity for relational roots to grow deep enough to matter. Most pastors have come to realize they can plan for new members to be a part of the church for only two to five years before these members may move again. So prevalent is this mobility phenomenon that most people assume a new relationship isn't going to last long before one or the other of them (or both) moves away. "So why bother getting started in the first place," the thinking goes. While at times we must face realities that require a move, we must learn to value the benefits of stability and longevity—characteristics that give community a real chance to succeed.

Set Geographic Boundaries

In a typical suburb, individual homes are clearly defined spaces. Therefore, one of the easiest steps you can take to create community in a suburban setting is to use those spaces to create your own geographic boundaries. Using your home as its center, scope out a one-mile radius around your home. (For people who live in rural areas or places with greater land mass, as in Texas, the circle may need to be a little bigger.) Make this area your place of concentration. For most suburban areas this will include anywhere from one hundred to two hundred homes. In urban settings, you may want to select an apartment community or take time to discover the historic or traditional "neighborhood" boundaries that exist around you. Seek to do as much within this radius as possible. Shop in this zone. Send your children to schools there. Most important, concentrate your Christian community development within this circle.

Identify a Core

Bring the matter to God in prayer and then seek out one or two Christian families in your neighborhood that you would like to get to know better. While it isn't absolutely essential that these families attend the same church you attend, there is at least one positive benefit if they do. Being connected during the week to the same body of Christians with whom you worship on the weekend gives you that much more in common. In our current neighborhood in San Antonio, we enjoy Christian fellowship with 58 of the 150 homes in our neighborhood. While several of these 58 households attend our church on the weekend, about five other churches are represented in the neighborhood. We see this as a wonderful expression of the body of Christ.

Free Up Your Schedule

Over the next six months, begin to free up your schedule. Make a master list of the things you do, and start saying no to what splinters your life and leaves you feeling hurried and stressed. This will mean you will say no to some of the things you enjoy, which will be hard to do. It will involve eliminating some — not all — of your children's sports commitments and other activities, and that will be hard to do as well. It will require you to delete some of your online accounts — though once they're gone, you'll likely never miss them. It will entail backing out of some of your own commitments — even church commitments, such as serving on committees. The truth is, these "good" commitments can pull you away from an experience of deep community as effectively as secular commitments can.

As you make these changes, others may ask why you're no longer involved in these activities. Tell them you are trying to simplify your life. Most will appreciate your effort. Be careful, however, not to preach to others or try to persuade them to do the same; a significant number of people won't get it or won't want this simplified schedule for themselves, and you are almost guaranteed to offend them in some way or another. I learned this the hard way. Go to school on my experience.

Spend Time Together

Begin spending time together with the one to two families or singles you have sought out in your neighborhood or apartment community. Start by sharing a dinner where everyone brings something. The combined effort should prevent anyone from feeling too stressed, but if it doesn't, keep adjusting your arrangements until any unnecessary stress is avoided. If you can't do dinner, do dessert. Take walks together in the neighborhood. (A word of caution: your neighbors may call the police to check out these "strangers" making their way through the neighborhood without workout gear and iPods!) The list of possibilities is unlimited. And the beauty of it is that community doesn't have to cost a lot of money. You can rent a classic movie and watch it together on a Friday night. If three families share the cost, it's even cheaper!

Agree to a Common Purpose

A common place is the best facilitator of community, but it does not guarantee community. Achieving community requires a common purpose. And for a community to be biblical, the common purpose must be biblical. Talk to your church leaders about the purposes, goals, or mission they would like to see you embrace; by doing so, it enables you to be connected to the broader body of Christ in your community. Look back over chapters 4 and 5 for assistance in establishing this vital component.

Play in the Front Yard Together

Many suburban homes today are built with porches, but they are mere facades. They look like a place where people hang out to talk and laugh, but seldom, if ever, is anyone found there. One of the simplest and most practical things you can do to create community in your neighborhood is to spend time on your front porch — or even play out in the front yard. While many suburban neighborhoods don't have sidewalks because of a lack of meaningful places to walk to — and because the streets are designed to serve cars, not people — it is still possible to rediscover the front of the house (and even the streets of neighborhoods) as the new hangout for the family.

Purchase lawn chairs or a swing, and sit on your porch or in the front yard in the evenings and on weekends. Sociologists have dubbed these front yard spaces as "micro-parks." Bring out a jug of iced tea with some extra glasses. It may take a while for others to catch on, but be patient. Play kickball in the streets. A neighbor might on occasion complain that the ball landed in their petunias, but eventually they'll join in the festivities. Wave to people driving by in their cars; one day they'll stop by. Have other Christian families in your neighborhood stop by for a visit. Invite children in the neighborhood to join in whatever game or activity that happens to be going on. A cul-de-sac makes for one of the best layouts for these activities, but it is not essential to enjoy an experience of community in the front yard. If you're in an apartment community, by all means use the clubhouse or pool area.

ORIENT YOURSELVES TO THE RULES OF BEING A GOOD NEIGHBOR

Make it a goal to find favor with your neighbors because of the kindness and character of your life.[17] Here are a handful of guiding principles:

- Take care of your property. If you don't do it for yourself, at least do it for your neighbors.
- Follow the ten-minute rule. Stop by to see neighbors spontaneously, but don't stay more than ten minutes. People who haven't yet restructured their lives will love to see you but likely won't have time for an unplanned visit. If you stop by to see a neighbor and find them working on a project, don't allow them to stop working, even if they say it's OK. In fact, the best thing to do is pitch in to help — assuming you know what you're doing!
- Muzzle the dog. If your dog barks all the time, come up with a solution. This happened to us years ago. Our relationally driven beagle hated it when we left and she was quarantined to the backyard. Apparently, she barked nonstop, but only until she heard us pull in the driveway. So we

never heard her. Our next-door neighbor worked out of his
house and was overcome with the whooping sound of our
hound. He finally mustered up the courage to tell us about
it. Our vet recommended a barking collar, which put an
end to the disturbance. The best news is that I maintain to
this day a great friendship with that neighbor. Barking dogs
may not bother you, but I know for sure they will bother
your neighbors.

- Put yourself in a place of need. Borrow stuff from your
  neighbors: a cup of sugar, jumper cables, a power washer.
  It gives you a great excuse to see them. Make sure when
  you return something (a tool, for example), it's cleaner than
  when you borrowed it. If you break it, replace it with something comparable. Return the favor and allow and even
  encourage neighbors to use your "stuff." My next-door
  neighbor and I have granted each other unlimited garage
  access to borrow tools.

- Use common sense. Don't play your music so loud that
  it disturbs your neighbor. Get permission to cut down a
  tree in your neighbor's yard before you go ahead and do it.
  Don't paint your house purple.

- Here is a novel idea: "Do to others what you would have
  them do to you."[18]

FIND A PURPOSE TO BRING ALL
THE NEIGHBORS TOGETHER

Find something the neighbors can rally around to make the neighborhood a better place to live. Petition to get a stop sign installed.
Organize a neighborhood watch. Have an old-fashioned block
party. Designate each Wednesday "volleyball night" or "basketball night." All these activities take abundant amounts of interaction to pull off—just the thing you need to form the foundation
for community.

This kind of winsome, invasive Christian community is similar to the experience of the first-century Christians, an experience described by Yale professor Wayne Meeks:

> The Pauline Group's strong and intimate sense of belonging, their special beliefs and norms, their perception of their own discreteness from "the world" did not lead them to withdraw into the desert, like the Essences of Qumran. They remained in the cities and their members continued to go about their ordinary lives in the streets and neighborhoods, shops and agora. Paul and the other leaders did not merely permit this continued interaction as something inevitable; in several instances they positively encouraged it (1 Corinthians 5:9–13).[19]

The goal of this chapter is not to encourage people to move from the suburbs to small towns; the goal is to show people who are stuck in the isolated trap of linear friendships that they are not alone, that many people are doing radical and even desperate things to change their situation. The postmodern world is sick of the philosophy of "be an individual at all costs," and people everywhere are searching for answers. I encourage church leaders to take advantage of this shift in its early stages. Let the ultimate "we" organization show the way. But will individual Christians and the church catch the early wave of this wonderful opportunity, or will we once again wait until we are forced to meld into a new culture, losing the chance to shape the values and structures that will govern it?

Lyle Schaller suggests that many people, confronted with the facts of where we are and where we may be headed, will either "(a) engage in denial or (b) refute most of the points of discontinuity and the probable consequences."[20] Bob and Karen Johnson have a rare opportunity to break the usual pattern of Homo sapiens and adopt a "new" way of life that is as old as human existence. The question must be asked: How badly do they want it?

Part 3

CONNECTING TO COMMON POSSESSIONS

Chapter 9

THE PROBLEM OF CONSUMERISM

The breakdown of a common purpose and a common place over the last sixty years has embedded individualism as a way of life in America, as well as in most modern communities around the world. Without warning, individualism has bred the most intense isolation since the day Adam spent alone in the garden of Eden.

One additional obstacle to community has raised its ugly head out of the modal qualities of individualism and isolation, namely, consumerism. Consumerism is about consumption — the concentrated effort to purchase, acquire, and use up things to meet one's real and perceived needs and wants. While some forms of consumption are both necessary and permissible, when it is practiced in an environment where the individual is sovereign, consumption can easily become an imbalanced obsession that kills community.

One of consumerism's driving principles is the elevation of rights over responsibilities. The pursuit and protection of one's rights always win out over one's responsibility to his or her neighbor. People don't deliberately choose consumerism because they are more depraved than previous generations; it is merely a natural consequence of an individualistic culture. When community life is strong, everyone looks out for each other. We are our "brother's keeper." But when individualism reigns as the predominant way of life, there is no one looking out for you. You must take on this role for yourself, and it is a full-time job.

In both modes of life, the Golden Rule applies, but it is

defined and applied very differently. In community, the Golden Rule says, "Do to others as you would have them do to you."[1] In consumerism, the Golden Rule says, "Do to others before they do it to you," or even more instructive, "He who has the gold, rules." The notion is simple: "The more cash you have, the better positioned you are to protect your rights." In a community philosophy, Christ is at the center of our lives as the driving motivation and resource for the biblical definition of the Golden Rule. In a philosophy of consumption, money and getting our needs met are the driving motivations of our lives. Jesus helpfully reminds us that these two opposing philosophies cannot coexist; one will win out against the other.[2] Our culture today favors individualism, making it extremely difficult for the Christian to sustain a biblically informed allegiance to Christ. We can claim Christ as Lord, but actively loving God and our neighbor is typically subservient to meeting our own needs and wants. Many churches and individuals today even look to God to serve and sanctify their consumerism.

Consumerism is not merely the result of individualism and isolation; it also fuels the continuation of the "sovereign individual" ideology. Consumerism, individualism, and our growing isolation feed one another and keep us trapped in a vicious circle:

Consumerism seeks to curb the negative feelings of isolation, and so we spend increasing amounts of money in an attempt to feel better. Yet, the more we consume as a solution to our loneliness, the more this feeds our individualistic idolatries.

CONSUMERISM AND COMMUNITY

Consumerism, in combination with our cultural individualism and isolation, can have a devastating effect on our attempts to build genuine community. Consumerism undermines community in at least four significant ways.

Imbalanced Independence

Consumerism tempts us into a form of independence. John Locke puts it succinctly when he writes, "If we needed things we couldn't buy, many of us would have more friendships."[3] The pursuit and attainment of Western wealth has enabled us to bypass each other as we pursue meeting our basic needs. Poet and farmer Wendell Berry observes, "If people don't need each other, they will spend little time together telling stories to each other, and if they don't know one another's stories, how can they know whether or not to trust one another?"[4] This experience of not needing each other leads to the second way in which consumerism destroys community.

Distrust

Our isolation creates a distorted view of the people who live around us. If our impressions of people are formed by stereotypes based on the nightly news or blogs on the Internet, we may not have an accurate view of the people who live around us. Television news, talk radio, and online blogs can leave us with the impression that most people are immoral and manipulative. We begin to view everyone we do not know (which is almost everyone we see) through suspicious eyes. We begin to assume that friendliness from a stranger comes with a self-promoting agenda. With this attitude as our starting point, our chances of achieving true community are squelched.

Lawsuits

Consumerism is driven by a preoccupation to meet one's needs and to protect one's property and rights—because, after all, if we don't, no one else will. Therefore, it should come as no surprise to learn that there has been a significant increase in the number of lawsuits filed over the last sixty years. The community ideology Jesus promoted suggests that if someone asks you to walk one mile with them, go two; if someone wants to sue you and take your shirt, give your coat as well; if someone slaps you on the cheek, turn and offer the other.[5] But how many Christians live this way today? In fact, the apostle Paul's teaching on lawsuits among believers sounds almost passé today:

> If any of you has a dispute with another, do you dare to take it before the ungodly for judgment instead of before the Lord's people? Or do you not know that the Lord's people will judge the world? And if you are to judge the world, are you not competent to judge trivial cases? Do you not know that we will judge angels? How much more the things of this life! Therefore, if you have disputes about such matters, do you ask for a ruling from those whose way of life is scorned in the church? I say this to shame you. Is it possible that there is nobody among you wise enough to judge a dispute between believers? But instead, one brother takes another to court—and this in front of unbelievers!
>
> The very fact that you have lawsuits among you means you have been completely defeated already. Why not rather be wronged? Why not rather be cheated? Instead, you yourselves cheat and do wrong, and you do this to your brothers and sisters.[6]

You may think Paul is naive. But in truth, his words are filled with rich principles that lead to life, love, and healthy community for those who obey them. They seem ridiculous only because they are built on a foundation radically different from individualism and unabashed consumerism. Ultimately, our mutual distrust and reliance on lawsuits to solve disputes with one another will kill the very economy that feeds our consumerism. Long-lasting economic development must be built on a foundation of trust, win-win proposals, and sacrifices, which are bedrock truths of healthy community.

Social Loafing

In a culture of individualism, people stop looking out for each other. And when this happens, the needs of the poor, the homeless, and the broken go unmet. In the absence of self-sacrificial love for one's neighbor, the government may seem to be the only solution for society's problems. But for a government to help, it must tax the people to fund its programs. Often, these government-funded programs are initiated with good motives but typically produce poor results. Even worse, the rise of government involvement leads people who could otherwise effectively serve to say, "I pay taxes for the government to take care of this!" This abdication of social responsibility is a disease John Locke refers to as "social loafing."[7] Sadly, this kind of sedentary apathy leads to atrophy of our muscles of human justice and kindness—a condition that is difficult to reverse in a culture of consumerism, even in the community of the church. In fact, those muscles can die and rigor mortis can set in.

LIFE-STAGE MARKETING

A culture of consumerism requires the presence of vendors who, in the modality of individualism, will market to the needs of the individual. The products and services they offer, undergirded by intense marketing horsepower, seek to feed our egos and satisfy our perceived needs and wants. But in the end they also divide us. Rarely does the American family do things together. Everyone is divided into a segment of the market, so much so that the family nucleus now is no longer a simple community but a detached collection of individuals. In the last sixty years, the church as a whole has bought into this method. By and large, successful churches are no longer building community; they simply market their consumable services to different individuals.

It's easy to see how the Johnson family is caught in the trap of consumerism. Consumerism is not based on the amount of money we have to spend; it's rooted in the *way we think* about the amount of money we have to spend. The Johnsons, like many of us, have lived under the grip of this lifestyle for most of their lives. In America, our fundamental picture of success is *accumulating more things.* And when the things we have just purchased do not bring relief from our isolation and our loneliness, we begin to look at others who, on the outside, appear happier and have more—or better—things than we do. We set a goal to purchase still more items, more often than not by plunking down our credit cards in a misguided effort to feel whole. The Bible says that covetousness, evil desires, greed, and such things are idolatry.[8]

When we pursue as our means of fulfillment the things our neighbor possesses instead of pursuing God, we worship these things rather than God alone. We were warned of this trap all the way back when God gave us the Ten Commandments. "You shall not covet your neighbor's house. You shall not covet your neighbor's wife, or his male or female servant, his ox or donkey, or anything that belongs to your neighbor."[9] The modern paraphrase of this ancient axiom may be, "Don't try to keep up with the Joneses." Now we see in full bloom that covetousness and greed also rob us of community. Instead of pursuing the joy of a conversation, we pursue the purchase of plastic or metal objects in varying sizes. This all-consuming pursuit pulls us away from the time-consuming pursuit of community. The popular quotation sums it up well: "We love things and use people instead of loving people and using things."

Given the condition of our society, it will take great courage and intentionality to choose a different path, because to do so means we will have to be countercultural. Speaking from an architectural, urban-planning point of view nearly thirty years ago, Philip Langdon offered this pessimistic prediction for the future, which, sadly, rings quite true today:

> It will not be easy to bring this vision of suburban design to fruition. The idea of a compact, mixed, affordable, pedestrian-scale community has emerged at a time when there is still a great deal of wealth in the United States, especially in the top fifth of the population. Surplus wealth enables people to persist in building wasteful, inadequate communities and then compensate for the communities' failings by buying private vehicles and driving all over the metropolitan area in search of what ought to be available close to home. The satisfying community designs of earlier times were dictated to a considerable extent by scarce resources. People supported neighborhood stores, and relied on sidewalks to get to and from the stores, because they didn't have the money and cars that would allow them to shop at big stores dispersed along distant roads. People lived at higher densities—and enjoyed a robust neighborhood life—because they could not afford detached houses on large lots in subdivisions many miles from their place of work. People settled in compact, relatively self-sufficient communities because the economy permitted little extravagance. One complication for today's traditionalists, then, lies in advocating a more efficient, compact community before the economy has made it necessary for the nation as a whole to adopt such a thrifty outlook. Thus it is possible that most suburban development in the United States will continue for some time on the profligate course it has followed since the Second World War.[10]

On a more positive note, Christianity has a long history of overcoming obstacles and swimming against the current. Bob and Karen Johnson are Christians; thus they have the power within them through Jesus Christ to make it happen. If you are a devoted follower of Christ, so do you.[11]

Now, on to practical solutions.

Chapter 10

CHARACTERISTICS OF COMMON POSSESSIONS

An exceedingly rich alternative to consumerism can be recommended to the Johnson family, one best described in the writings of Luke as he peers into the community of the first-century Christians and his gaze locks on a man named Barnabas:

> All the believers were one in heart and mind. No one claimed that any of their possessions was their own, but they shared everything they had. With great power the apostles continued to testify to the resurrection of the Lord Jesus. And God's grace was so powerfully at work in them all that there were no needy persons among them. For from time to time those who owned land or houses sold them, brought the money from the sales and put it at the apostles' feet, and it was distributed to anyone who had need.
>
> Joseph, a Levite from Cyprus, whom the apostles called Barnabas (which means "son of encouragement"), sold a field he owned and brought the money and put it at the apostles' feet.[1]

In direct contrast to the example of Barnabas is the story that immediately follows in Acts 5: "Now a man named Ananias, together with his wife Sapphira, also sold a piece of property. With his wife's full knowledge he kept back part of the money for himself, but brought the rest and put it at the apostles' feet."[2] The problem with Ananias and Sapphira wasn't that they hadn't turned over the full proceeds from their land sale; the problem was that they gave everyone the impression they had given it all when in fact they hadn't. They wanted the public glory of being sacrificial givers for the sake of others, but their own selfishness was at the core of their motive, and the truth came out.

This is a poignant peek into the darkness of consumerism. While the actions of Ananias and Sapphira may have looked selfless and sacrificial, it was clear their actions were motivated by selfish gain. This serves as a great reminder that regardless of our actions, we must first bring our hearts before God and ask him to test our motives. We will never experience true community just because people give up their resources for others. But when people give up their resources because the power of the resurrection of Jesus Christ has penetrated their lives, they are overwhelmed by the grace that leads to a lifestyle of generous giving.

This paves the way for a final suggestion for creating authentic Christian community: *share common possessions.* "No one claimed that any of their possessions was his own, but they shared everything they had."[3] This doesn't mean the early believers simply pooled their resources together. It appears everyone maintained ownership of their own possessions, but they were more than willing to share or sell what they had so those in need would be cared for. The mind-set was this: All that we are, everything that we own, belongs to God.[4] He is the owner; we are merely the managers, the stewards. We must remain open to God's leadership, asking him how he wants us to use his resources, how he wants us to spend our very lives. We ask such questions as, "What would Jesus want me to do with my car, my swimming pool, my lawn mower, this extra cash I have?"

Respected theologian and scholar Martin Marty once quoted the late Yale professor-preacher Halford Luccock, who reflected on the insidious power of money over the hearts of Christians:

> You remember that among the Franks, whole armies were sometimes given baptism at one stroke, and many warriors went into the water with their right hands held high so that

they did not get wet. Then they could say, "This hand has never been baptized," and they could swing their battle axes just as freely as ever. The modern counterpart of that partial baptism is seen in many people who have been baptized, all except their pocket-books. They held these high out of the water.[5]

Many Christians today hold their wallets out of the water so they can continue in their own minds to maintain ownership over and control of their possessions and to accumulate more possessions. To be clear, I'm not saying God is *against* Christians having money, seeking to earn more money, or even enjoying possessions. As long as these things have been secured within biblical and ethical boundaries and the follower of Christ is devoting his or her time and talents to that which they truly believe God is leading them to do, God will be honored. What is of utmost importance is this: believing that "man shall not live on bread alone, but on every word that comes from the mouth of God."[6] We must understand that Jesus is "the bread of life" that God has provided for us.[7] Once again, it comes down to putting Christ at the center of life, over our desire for and commitment to money.

Money and possessions, in submission to Christ, are wonderful tools and resources given by God to be used to achieve his objectives. Think of a man or woman who owns a company but decides to turn over ownership to someone who has greater resources and capital while he or she stays on as the CEO. This is how our relationship with God works when it comes to our worldly assets. We acknowledge God as the true owner who has far greater resources than we could ever dream of possessing. We are given a prominent position in the company as CEO, but God remains the owner.

But this isn't just about money. Christian stewardship, or life management, involves not only money and physical possessions. God wants all of our gifts, our talents, and our time. Healthy Christian community will demonstrate five characteristics when the principles of godly stewardship of our possessions, time, and talents are being lived out.

FIVE CHARACTERISTICS OF COMMUNITY AROUND COMMON POSSESSIONS

I suggest at least five characteristics can be found in effective places of community.

Interdependency

For the past fifty years, the typical goal in American society has been achieving independence. Even work among the poor has typically focused on helping to make them independent and self-reliant. Independence implies self-sufficiency, usually accompanied by an adequate cash flow that enables a person to function in life without the aid of others. While the proverb "Give a person a fish and you feed him for a day; teach a person how to fish and you feed him for a lifetime" is helpful, a better goal is to help others not so they can become independent but so they can become contributing members of an interdependent community. We want to help others so they can help others, creating a community that cares for the needs of its members.

Social programs that keep people dependent on "picking up fish each day" are clearly not the solution. Overt dependence on others is never healthy. But neither is it wise to promote unmitigated independence. The air of independence encourages and fuels individualism, isolation, and consumerism and fails to solve the long-term social problems that fuel poverty and the lack of resources in a community. Instead, we should encourage the growth of *interdependent* relationships. In these relationships, individuals choose to make their resources available to others instead of choosing to consume all they can for themselves, either through accumulating vast savings or through purchasing all kinds of amenities.

Paul summarizes this mind-set in his letter to the Corinthians, who lived in the booming and progressive country of Greece:

> Our desire is not that others might be relieved while you are hard pressed, but that there might be equality. At the present time your plenty will supply what they need, so that in turn their plenty will supply what you need. The goal is equality, as it is written: "The one who gathered much did not have too much, and the one who gathered little did not have too little."[8]

For the Johnsons, this may mean they evaluate their current resources (money, possessions, time, and talents) to determine together how God wants them to use these resources to show love for him and neighbor. This attitude will also serve as a filter through which they sift future decisions about how to spend their time and what they purchase. Now, instead of always asking what will make *them* happy, they are principally concerned with what will please God.

This doesn't mean they are committing to an austere, dreary lifestyle. It is amazing to see how God will sometimes smile at us and nudge us to "treat" ourselves to things that bring great pleasure. We are his children, after all, and he truly delights to see us enjoy life. Yet, more than anything else, he wants us to be obedient.[9] The biblical precept is simple: Truly delight yourself in God, "and he will give you the desires of your heart."[10] Study the Scriptures and learn from them what brings delight to the heart of God. If you choose to do this, one of two things will happen: either you will find that as you grow in your love for and delight in God and the things he loves, he will change what you desire, or out of the pleasure he derives from your spiritual maturity and trustworthiness, he will give you what brings you pleasure.

One of the reasons God may not give us greater responsibility at work, open the way for us to get larger raises, or provide us with more possessions, however, is that we may not have proven to be trustworthy stewards with what he has already given us: "From everyone who has been given much, much will be demanded; and from the one who has been entrusted with much, much more will be asked."[11]

In the Old Order Amish communities in states such as Ohio and Pennsylvania, a high value is placed on interdependence. When a barn needs to be built, the family does not flaunt its independence and success by hiring a contractor. Rather, they organize a "barn raising" in which all community members come together to share a big meal and to build the barn. Because many Amish men are skilled craftsmen who are in high demand in the non-Amish suburbs, they could certainly afford to outsource many of their projects. But they choose not to because it would undermine and diminish their community, which is of far more value than having time for themselves.

The average American can easily build a life in which they don't need anyone—a life of complete independence. But simply because we *can* do this doesn't mean we *should*. Interdependence is a choice we make. Negotiating this value in an era of abundant wealth will be difficult, but it is essential to developing a community in which we truly "belong" to one another. Belonging implies a sense of ownership, a sense that we are related to one another in dependent, yet healthy ways. James Howard Kunstler sums it up this way: "Community is not something you have, like a pizza; it is a local organism based on a web of interdependencies."[12]

Intergenerational Life

Another dynamic characteristic found among inspiring places of community is intergenerational life. In all places of effective community, with the possible exception of college life, the various strata of generations spend both structured and spontaneous time together. Intergenerational life isn't a luxury to be tried just to see if we like it, to decide if it's "cool." No, it is essential for members of true community to grow and mature.

Each generation has much to offer the others. The child instills a wonderful sense of purpose into older generations, encouraging them to serve as those who dispense the lessons of life they have learned over the years. The young single person renews our passion for spirited ideals, vision, and hope. What's more, they're also wonderful mentors for our children because they have the energy to simply "hang with them," and our children tend to look up to them. Parents carry the responsibility of being the principal providers and guides for their children. And finally, we must never forget that the elderly have much to offer, not only because they have learned many of the timeless lessons about life, but because they bring a perspective often refreshingly free from the tyranny of the daily "to do" list. Those who have gained wisdom that comes with age can look at life from a broad, global perspective and share lessons learned from years of personal experience.

Christian community is not an occasional group get-together led by small group leaders; it is at its core a familial structure. It is patriarchal and matriarchal in structure. It is a way of life one is trained to participate in by those who are older, over the course of life through all the stages of life.[13] But because we have tended to be segmented into tightly defined life-stage groupings, even in the church, this view of community requires an unusual type of training — one never meant for a classroom but experienced throughout the course of everyday life.

Many church leaders have been trained to believe that the most effective grouping of people is around common life-stage experience. While this may be the *fastest* way to grow a group of people numerically, it doesn't necessarily produce the best qualitative results in the lives of individuals. Putting a group of five young married couples with small children in a room together and expecting them to help each other navigate these crucial and sometimes exasperating years is a bit like asking a group of ten toddlers to brainstorm ways to cross a four-lane highway together! Age-based affinity is powerfully attractive, but it can lead to long-term problems.

The life-stage mind-set is so ingrained that it has a powerful effect on America's youngest members as well as its oldest. As our children grow up, many aren't comfortable relating to people of other ages. Furthermore, so devastating can life-stage grouping be that, according to some reports, the highest rate of suicide in the United States is among the elderly.[14] It can be painful to live without the kind of vital, lasting purpose that comes from being part of an intergenerational community.

Is it possible we could see a cultural shift from life-stage community to intergenerational community at some point in our lifetime? On the positive side, the growing value of intergenerational life is being recognized by young adults in their twenties. Driven by postmodern values, they seem to be crying out for it. Dieter and Valerie Zander, pastors and Baby Boomer mentors to Gen Xers, have said, "The potentially endless proliferation of new subgroups begins to look like it is based on nothing more substantial than catering to new styles. That kind of shallowness won't last."[15]

Will new generations succeed in bridging the generational gaps we have created? I believe those of us who are older have a real opportunity to begin building this mind-set into our children and grandchildren, introducing them to the experiences of intergenerational community. The challenge that remains is changing the deeply embedded structures and patterns of our culture. How can we effectively pass down to the next generation a way of life that we ourselves don't understand? We may not succeed for a generation or two, but if change is to happen, it must begin today.

Children

If we seek out and value intergenerational community, then we must understand the role of children and our adult responsibilities for them in a community. Effective and healthy communities accept the responsibility to help parents care for, nurture, and train their children, who in turn learn a way of life that counters the isolation of individualism.

The American suburban life that features parents working outside the home and no other family available has created "latchkey children." Movies like *Suburbia* depict the tragic reality of the resulting isolation experienced by many children. In the absence of being effectively cared for by their parents—whether in a latchkey situation or another form of adolescent isolation— kids may eventually create their own communities in gangs, for mostly unhealthy purposes, uniting around a common need to belong. In urban areas, gangs establish geographic boundaries, designating turf they will defend. In the suburbs, gangs may not seek to possess geographic regions, but they congregate online or in local malls. As long as we propagate dysfunctional families, it is conceivable that we will continue to propagate such dysfunctional community.

In the average American small group experience, children are also typically left out. In some cases, group members may not be able to even name the children of fellow members. And sadly, many children in Christian families hate small group night because it takes their parents away from them. The irony is that the kids are left with a babysitter so Mom and Dad can go to a small group to talk about their children, with 90 percent of the prayer requests centering around everybody's busy schedules *or their concerns about their children.*

When asked about including children in a small group experience, the responses of most group members sound like a broken record: "We tried it, and it didn't work." "It's too chaotic." "The adults don't enjoy it as much." The role of children in the life of the community is dismissed as though it is as optional as leather seats in a new vehicle. But what if excluding children was not optional? Though including children can present some challenges, it has healthy, long-term benefits. Children learn what it means to follow God by seeing the pattern of discipleship modeled by adults who live in community together. And in effective places of genuine Christian community, spiritual grandparents, aunts, uncles, cousins, nieces, and nephews—all intimately involved in the lives of the children—support parents in ways most small groups cannot.

Indeed, it does take a village—a neighborhood, in fact—

to help Mom and Dad raise a balanced and healthy child. We may well wonder whether we're choosing ineffective and possibly damaging substitutes for a wholesome, effective intergenerational community — like latchkey isolation and babysitters while parents attend small group meetings without their children.

Responsibility

In a culture of individualism, protecting one's own rights and meeting one's own needs reign supreme. In a culture of true community, the opposite is true. While the individual certainly does — and should — take care of himself or herself in community, priority is given to serving and caring for others. Biblical community is built on the words of the apostle Paul:

> If you have any encouragement from being united with Christ, if any comfort from his love, if any common sharing in the Spirit, if any tenderness and compassion, then make my joy complete by being like-minded, having the same love, being one in spirit and of one mind. Do nothing out of selfish ambition or vain conceit. Rather, in humility value others above yourselves, not looking to your own interests but each of you to the interests of the others.
>
> In your relationships with one another, have the same mindset as Christ Jesus.[16]

When someone is suffering or gripped by despair, the other members see their involvement not as optional but as a duty that must be exercised if community is to work — and to work for them when they are the ones hurting. Remember, though, that the commitment to serve others is not made just because you want others, in time, to reach out to serve you. In Christ's community, where members are truly in fellowship with God, you are supernaturally led to pour out love on others:

> This is how we know what love is: Jesus Christ laid down his life for us. And we ought to lay down our lives for our brothers and sisters. If anyone has material possessions and sees a

brother or sister in need but has no pity on them, how can the love of God be in that person? Dear children, let us not love with words or speech but with actions and in truth.

This is how we know that we belong to the truth and how we set our hearts at rest in his presence: If our hearts condemn us, we know that God is greater than our hearts, and he knows everything.[17]

Love for God and love for others go hand in hand. Followers of Christ just can't help expressing their love for God through loving others. Those traits that are growing in their hearts must find an external outlet. When we discover true community, the place where responsibility toward others is a higher priority than standing up for our own rights, we will never want to go back. And it is amazingly freeing when others look out for us, pick us up when we have fallen, genuinely applaud our accomplishments, and lovingly confront us when we career off track.

Self-promotion is ultimately a most unfulfilling and exhausting way to live.

Sacrifice

The final characteristic of the kind of community that promotes common possessions and negates consumerism is sacrifice. Sacrifice is responsibility taken to the next level — often a deeply painful and costly level. Most of the time, we can execute responsibility in a way that does not challenge us; we merely draw on our physical, emotional, and financial reserves. From time to time, however, we are called to dig deep into who we are and what we have so that in the end we become depleted in a significant way for the sake of someone else. Eberhard Arnold states it well:

In the human body, community is maintained only by the constant cycle of dying cells being replaced by new ones. In a similar way, a life of full community can take shape as an organism only where there is heroic sacrifice. Because it is an educational fellowship of mutual help and correction, of shared resources, and of work, a true community is a covenant made in free-willing surrender and sacrifice. As such it fights for the existence of the church.[18]

It is at this point that effective Christian community breaks with effective non-Christian community. To achieve this objective of sacrificial service, one must truly be in fellowship with God; one must truly draw on the rich resources of the Holy Spirit within. When a great sacrifice has been made, the Christ follower learns firsthand what Jesus meant when he said, "Whoever wants to be my disciple must deny themselves and take up their cross and follow me. For whoever wants to save their life will lose it, but whoever loses their life for me will find it."[19]

In the late nineteenth century, the German social theorist Ferdinand Tönnies coined two words for community: *gemeinschaft* and *gesellschaft*. *Gemeinschaft* stands for the true community that flows from natural, emotional, and interdependent associations among people. It has become a catchphrase for the old "village community"—homogenous, interdependent, and close-knit. *Gesellschaft*, on the other hand, represents a contrived community characterized by the rational and instrumental associations we create. It is also a catchphrase for the impersonal, alienated, mobile, modern culture that has replaced *gemeinschaft*.[20] Sadly, many people will try to pawn off *gesellschaft* for *gemeinschaft*. Even the church does this (unknowingly for the most part). But, as Eberhard Arnold suggests, "efforts to organize community artificially can only result in ugly, lifeless caricatures."[21]

The Johnsons have had all they can take of *gesellschaft*; they are ready for *gemeinschaft*. As we look in on them again, they are taking the plunge into biblical community. They know it won't be easy, but the alternative is year after year after year of the same lonely, unsatisfying experience. As they prepare to seek authentic community, they know they've been spared much loss and tragedy to this point in their lives. But the next season of their life may well include caring for aging parents and coping with the reality that one or all of their parents will soon die. They may have to deal with a major illness that strikes one of them or a family member, or perhaps they'll have to cope with the results of an accident. And as their children enter adolescence, the Johnsons will have to adjust to the need for their kids to become more independent. They also worry about the possibility that an unstable economy will negatively affect their current financial prosperity.

If and when any of these challenges come, the Johnsons do not want to face them alone. But they are driven by more than just needing to find comfort in the midst of the storms. They long for the joy that comes from being connected to the body of Christ in an authentic and rich way. They can sense that when their purpose in life is linked to the whole, they can achieve far more than they can on their own. The Johnsons are coming to see the wisdom in the lesson learned from geese: Like a flock of geese in a V formation, they can go much farther each day (70 percent farther for the geese) by "flying" together than by venturing out on their own.

How about you? Perhaps the best thing you can do right now is set down this book and ask God to guide you in discerning his will and in showing you practical steps to embark on your search for true community. In whatever way seems appropriate, demonstrate that your life is open for reinventing. Then read the next chapter to find out what the Johnsons are experiencing just two years after devoting themselves to a community of believers who are committed to a common purpose, a common place, and common possessions.

Chapter 11
REDISCOVERING AUTHENTIC COMMUNITY

The time came for the Johnsons to make some changes. They realized the way they were living just wasn't working and decided to give this adventure called biblical community a try. As they saw it, they had little to lose and a lot to gain! They found that even more than a desire to *own* things or *do* things, they had a desire to *be* like a certain person—to be like Jesus. And they came to realize that the only way to grow to be like Jesus is to be involved and embedded in community with other people who are also committed to following him—*together*.

The Johnsons knew they could make minor, helpful adjustments in their lifestyle that would allow them to feel less stressed and more comfortable. But they wisely concluded that even with these adjustments, they could not sacrifice the basic principles of Scripture—the ways of life and discipleship that lead to genuine biblical community. They knew if they merely tried to modify their current dysfunctional lifestyle, they would eventually diminish the quality of relationships and simplicity of life they longed for deeply. Some, if not most, people choose the road of incremental steps when making lifestyle changes. For the Johnsons, however, this was a decision to go "all in." They sensed it was time to take the plunge.

Coming to this decision together as a family took several rounds of discussions at family meetings and a lot of prayer, but they finally began to make aggressive moves toward pursuing their dream of connectedness. They were greatly motivated by a vision for a different kind of life for their children. Buoyed by this hope for a better way of life, they courageously moved ahead, even when fear threatened to overwhelm them and stop them in their tracks.

As you read the next few pages and observe some of the steps they took to change, keep in mind that your own journey into authentic community will undoubtedly look different from their journey. I encourage you to see the story of the Johnsons as an opportunity to discover and learn from them as pioneers. Then, with God's help and direction, grab your spiritual machete and blaze your own path.

COMMIT TO A COMMON PURPOSE

The first decision Bob and Karen had to make was to simply begin. But where? They chose to first embrace the common purpose God had laid out for them (and us) in his Word. They began to talk about how they could better align their own stories as individuals and a family to God's story. They studied the Scriptures, and in Genesis 3 they learned about God's ultimate vision to restore what had been lost in the garden of Eden. They began to better understand God's desire to come down to be with us, to dwell inside of us, to do life with us, to take walks with us in the cool of the day. They saw that God wants us to experience the perfect community of the Father, Son, and Holy Spirit. They understood that God's first priority for us is not "to do" but "to be" — to be like Jesus, full of grace and truth, in our relationships with each other.

The Johnsons learned that as people who have been forgiven and accepted into the family of God on the basis of the sacrificial death and resurrection power of Jesus, they were now called to align their lives with the life of God by joining in community with other believers. Together, the followers of Jesus form his body on earth, to be a visible witness to the world, continuing the plan of God begun in Christ in the power of the Holy Spirit. This means the Johnsons can't just "go it alone." They must commit to doing life with a small band of believers, representing Jesus together.

The Johnsons also made a colossal decision to trade their goal of accumulation for conversation, exchange doing for being, and swap success for faithfulness. They embraced these paradigm shifts with confidence in the teaching of Jesus, who urges us to "seek first his kingdom and his righteousness, and all these things will be given to you as well."[1] They held fast to this promise — that if they would align their lives to God's kingdom purposes as their first priority and preoccupation in life, God would give them many of the things that used to occupy first place in their lives.

The truth they are quickly discovering is that all the other "stuff" just doesn't matter as much as it used to. As the Johnsons began to give up their former idols, God was transforming them. The good things God provides now fit into their rightful place and can be freely enjoyed as gifts from God rather than as idols that can never deliver on their promises.

COMMIT TO A COMMON PLACE

While the Johnsons understand there are many different ways to join a small group of believers to live out God's call, they have chosen to embrace the vision of doing this with other believers in their local neighborhood. They have prayerfully decided to park the car and spend more evenings outside taking walks, sitting on their front porch, and "whiling away" the evening with their family and neighbors.

They know they will need to intentionally seek out one or two other homes in their neighborhood where believers in Jesus live who are willing to join them on this adventure. They are looking for a redefined small group experience. They want something that is different from the small groups they've known before. They are looking for a small group of believers:

- whom they naturally encounter just about every day because they share the same space (not just planned encounters at small group gatherings)
- who know each other and act as spiritual grandparents, aunts, and uncles to their children
- who are committed to growing together in all that it means to *be like Jesus*
- who are committed to collectively giving their lives to help other neighbors, to simply do what Jesus instructed us to do: "love your neighbor as yourself"
- who can join them in recreating, having fun, and simply hanging out

FINDING MARGIN IN FINANCES

Karen recently came across these verses in the book of Acts in her Bible reading and couldn't wait to share them with Bob:

> "God began by making one person, and from him came all the different people who live everywhere in the world. God decided exactly when and where they must live. God wanted them to look for him and perhaps search all around for him and find him, though he is not far from any of us."[2]

What a profound insight from the apostle Paul! As Karen read these words, she realized God had been intentional in planning for her and her family to be alive at this exact time in history. Not only that, he had in mind the exact place he intended for them to live. Why? So that when people they encounter are ready to seek him (especially those who are convinced God is distant and not involved in their lives), they will discover that he is actually quite near. He is visibly present in the lives of the Johnsons because they have joined their story to his.

Since God now makes his dwelling in believers who collec-

REDISCOVERING AUTHENTIC COMMUNITY   151

tively represent their risen Lord as the body of Christ, God is *not* far away. He is present and at work in the Johnsons' neighborhood because now, when people call out to God and seek him, they will find him through the witness of the Johnsons. It is a profound mystery how God works all this out, but the Johnsons are content to leave that part of the work to God.[3] They are simply available to be used by God when he is ready to do his work.

The Johnsons know some will see their next decision as a bit radical, but they have come to believe that God is calling them to move. Along with seeking God's face in dedicated prayer, two reasons underlie this decision. First, they are ready for a fresh start. They originally bought their home because of the internal amenities — granite countertops, stainless steel appliances, spacious rooms, a pool, separate living areas, walk-in closets, and a three-car garage. Now they realize they should have been more mindful of "the whom" than "the what." *Whom* was God calling them to love and serve?

The second force behind their decision to move is a matter of margin — specifically, *financial* margin. The Johnsons realize that to engage in this new way of life, they need to reclaim some financial margin. There is no way to simplify their lives unless they reduce the amount of money it takes to pay the bills. Bob and Karen embarrassingly confess that they are not funding a lifestyle of needs but a chosen lifestyle of wants. Downsizing from their "McMansion" to a smaller, adequately sized home will free up God's resources for greater involvement in his calling.

Three principles guide them as they follow through on this decision. First, they set a price range that will allow them to fund a mortgage on Bob's salary alone. Second, they look for a neighborhood that will cut down Bob's commute to work. And third, they look for a place where at least two families from their church live — giving them the possibility of forming a small group right in their neighborhood.

It takes several months to change their lives around, but when it all comes together, they are amazed at how satisfying this new way of life is for them. One thing that surprises them is how a smaller house helps the family spend more time together in the same room. Each step they have taken in faith has confirmed the rightness of their decision and given them courage to take the next step.

FINDING MARGIN IN TIME

The next major goal for the Johnsons is to find more margin in their *time*. Busyness is the greatest threat to the new way of life they have chosen. To make the greatest gains, the Johnsons decide that over the course of the next six months, Karen will transition from her current job to work she can do at home on their home computer. Because of her accounting background, she is able to contract with two small businesses to keep their books. Although the salary is considerably smaller, the savings they realize because of reduced needs — not as much gasoline, no after-school care, and less need for professional clothes — nearly make up the difference. Plus, with the mortgage being paid completely from Bob's salary, the adjustment isn't as difficult as they imagined it would be.

The biggest blessing in all of this has been additional time. Bob's office is now only five minutes away, giving him back five to ten hours a week, depending on traffic. Karen's commute is nonexistent. Not only does working at home give Karen back the seven and a half hours she once spent commuting; it gives her additional flexibility. She is now in a position to manage her day in a way that keeps family needs and responsibilities more in balance with her work. She is available to participate in her children's school activities without feeling guilty for taking time away from work. Her constant presence in the home has created a new sense of calm for everyone. Managing a home takes time, and beginning the process in the evening hours used to make life feel crazy and harried. Now the evening hours have become a period of refuge and replenishment for the entire family.

But the time margin increase hasn't stopped here. Sitting down as a family, the Johnsons made a list of all their commitments, putting a check mark next to the commitments that have been pulling them apart as a family and stealing the time they needed to build deep relationships with their new neighbors.

Two areas in particular are significantly adjusted. First, they cut back on several church activities. It isn't that these activities are bad; the problem is that they created fragmentation. The Bible study, men's group, and mission committee, for instance, are all great programs, but many of the goals of these ministries can now be accomplished within the confines of their neighborhood. With their friends in this small community of believers, Bob and Karen are now responding to God, studying the Bible together and reaching out right in their neighborhood. Serving together in this way deepens these relationships—a key to true transformation. Hours once given to fragmented activities are now being deposited back into the time bank.

The next category they trim down is children's activities. The Johnsons recognize that sports and organized activities for their children with children of the same age have their place and value. But for them, things had gotten out of control. As a family, they have decided that from now on, each child will be involved in only one extracurricular activity at a time and the activity will be family friendly and involve reasonable costs and time commitments. Instead of the select baseball team their son was invited to play on, costing $2,000 with fifty-five games over the summer, they have chosen the local parks league, with sixteen games and a cost of $35. To the parents' surprise, their son is elated to have more free time to roam the neighborhood, be creative, and catch his breath. Once again, hours are being added back into the time bank.

Karen's decision to work out of the home has also enabled her to pick up the children right after school rather than sending them to after-school programs. With a little extra discipline, she has been able to get the children settled down so they are able to complete their homework before dinner—at least on most days! Not only has this given them more time together as a family in the evening; it has greatly reduced the stress level in their home.

Make no bones about it, these changes haven't always been smooth or easy. They've been the result of lengthy conversations, and none of it happened overnight. But with each step they've taken, with each decision Bob and Karen have made, they have built momentum. Best of all, they now feel like they have regained some control and freedom in their lives. They are living out their values rather than struggling with guilt, anxiety, and disappointment, and living at the mercy of misplaced priorities.

INVEST NEW MARGIN ON LIVING

As the Johnsons have begun to settle into the radical changes they've made, they have also begun to reinvest some of this extra margin. This is where things have gotten interesting! First, the Johnsons set a goal of having dinner as a family at least three times a week, and much to their surprise, they now find they are averaging four to six times a week! They also have made it a priority to turn off their phones during dinner. No tweeting, texting, or checking Facebook at the table. Though the Johnsons don't know this, an extensive Columbia University study suggests that this decision to eat dinner together will do more to keep their children from involvement in gangs, premarital sex, drugs, and alcohol than any other decision they could make.[4] When our children know they have a seat at our table, they don't go looking for it elsewhere!

The Johnsons have also decided to put their work down for the day and be available for each other and their neighbors from dinnertime to bedtime. Two or three times a week, they share a meal or an after-dinner dessert with the two Christian families they know in their neighborhood. They talk and laugh together. They'll often nail down plans for getting together the next day or on the weekend—sometimes to watch a movie together on Friday evening, go on a golf outing or a campout, or take a leisurely stroll together through the neighborhood.

Bob and Karen have also installed a big swing in their front yard. Several nights a week, they sit outside with a cup of coffee or a glass of iced tea. Often they play Frisbee or get a game of kickball going in the street. The children in the neighborhood were the first to come out, asking their parents if they could play with the neighbors. The kids had so much fun they couldn't be pulled away, and eventually, the parents wandered over to accompany their kids home. They often lingered to talk, and in the process, Bob and Karen have come to know their new neighbors better than they ever knew any of their previous neighbors. They can't believe how simple it has been and how much they actually enjoy it. They've come to realize most of their new neighbors want the same things they do but are at a loss to know how to find it.

STARTING AN INTENTIONAL INTERGENERATIONAL GATHERING

After a year of living in their new neighborhood and engaging in this new way of life, the Johnsons decide to start a monthly gathering with other believers in their neighborhood. They believe it will allow them to be more intentional about their spiritual growth and will help coordinate meeting needs in their neighborhood and city, and it may even provide opportunities to help believers in other parts of the world.

They organize a dessert night and invite the two families that attend their church and three other Christian families from the neighborhood who attend other churches. It is good to spend time with members of God's universal church, and it is also good to experience the benefits of an intergenerational gathering. To their delight, all of the families accept the invitation. At the dessert they explain what they have in mind—a simple gathering once a month in which they join together in the spirit of the first church gathering in Acts 2:42–47. They talk about *belonging*

together by sharing a meal and enjoying each other's fellowship—
kids included. About *growing* together by simply reading a chapter from the Bible, discussing it, and spending time praying for
each other and for the needs of their neighbors. And about *serving* together by identifying needs in their neighborhood and then
with God's help meeting them to the best of their ability.

Everyone signs up with enthusiasm! The age span of the
group ranges from six months to sixty-five years, so it truly is
an intergenerational group, and the six families begin to meet
together on Sunday evenings. Again, there is nothing especially
complicated about their gathering.

- *They share a meal.* Everyone brings a dish or something to
  drink—an old-fashioned potluck of sorts. They start by
  getting in a circle and holding hands. The host for the evening offers a prayer of thanks for the meal, acknowledges
  Jesus' presence at their little gathering, and prays for God's
  blessings on the evening. The first hour is spent eating great
  food, catching up on life's ventures, laughing, and enjoying
  each other's company.
- *They read the Word.* After dinner, everyone makes his or
  her way to the living room where they sit on sofas, chairs,
  and the floor. They read a chapter in the Bible and discuss
  the application to their lives as they commit to becoming
  like Jesus for the sake of each other, their neighbors, and
  the world. They began reading in the book of James since
  it was likely the first New Testament book written. The
  group thought it would be interesting to read the New Testament letters in the order they were written to capture the
  progression of the early church's story.
- *They pray together.* The group decides to keep a journal of
  their prayer requests. Adults and children alike share personal requests. To encourage prayers for their neighbors,
  each person is invited to ask their other neighbors between
  gatherings how they can pray for them. A member of the

group, even a child, volunteers to pray for each specific request out loud until all requests are mentioned.

- *They seek to serve.* The last thing the group does is ask a simple question: "How is God calling us to serve our neighbors and community?" The only way to effectively answer this question is to know what is going on in the lives of their other neighbors. It may take some time to find a rhythm, but the group is committed to serving their neighbors in love.

BE OUTWARD FOCUSED

About seven months into the monthly gatherings, Tim told of a conversation he had with a woman who lives at the end of his street. Because he seldom saw her outside, it had been difficult to get to know her. In fact, he didn't even know her name. But as he was out walking the dog the previous week, Tim noticed she was standing in her driveway and decided to stop by for a visit.

In that single encounter he learned that her name is Patty and that Patty has a sad story. She has experienced a difficult divorce and now lives alone, and her grown children aren't speaking to her. On top of that, her job is barely covering her mortgage payments, and she is feeling overwhelmed with the responsibility of taking care of her house. She shared with Tim that she is feeling deeply depressed. The group prayed for Patty, and then one of the members of the group had an idea.

What if they could find a way to help Patty? After some discussion, the group decided they would tend to Patty's unkempt lawn and help her weed the flower beds. Tim was assigned to connect with Patty to see if she was OK with the idea. She agreed, with some hesitancy. After all, she did not know these people very well. After a month of planning and coordinating, the day came for the neighbors to gather at Patty's house. Everyone contributed some money to pay for new grass seed and sod (including the children, who set aside a portion of their allowance). Everyone had a job to do, from seeding the grass and laying out the sod to pulling weeds and bagging debris. Some helped make lunch, and others made trips to the local hardware store for additional supplies.

As the day of work came to an end and the yard was starting to shape up, Patty approached Bob and Tim and asked the obvious question. "Why? Why are you doing this?" Tim gave Patty an honest answer: "We are a group of Christians who live in your neighborhood, and we just wanted to love you the way Jesus does." With tears flowing down her face, Patty asked Tim another question: "May I join you?" Bob and Tim both answered at the same time: "Yes!"

Patty came to the next monthly gathering, and she hasn't missed one since. She even joined the group on their next service day to help another neighbor. Soon, it began to dawn on this little band of believers what God was up to in their neighborhood. He was doing *through them* what he had done through the early church in Acts and through his followers down through the centuries. As they gathered to belong and grow together, their increasing love as a community of Christ followers was now spreading outward to meet the needs of the people around them. As a result of their genuine, sincere love for one another and their desire to love others with the love of God, "the Lord added to their number."[5]

Clearly, this is just a brief description of what is possible when followers of Christ decide they want to live in a different way. It's a vision of a church that is *connected* — to one another, to their neighbors, and to God. More than simply being a program of the church, it's a vision of a transformed community living counterculturally, attracting notice from neighbors as a visible witness to God's love.

If we were to fast-forward the story of the Johnsons, you would likely see these results: they have grown deeper in their relationships; their community cares for each other through trials — sickness, death, job loss; and they continue to reach out to their neighbors, seeing more of them come to faith in Jesus and join another small group that will be the presence of Jesus in their neighborhood.

They have also begun to reach out to the broader community around them — to the local schools and to the organizations that work with the homeless and poor. Next, they hope to pool their resources and start working with an international organization that is transforming whole communities in the name of Christ through church planting, micro-lending, water well development, education, medical aid, and career training. Each step of the way, their children are involved in praying, giving, and sharing in the exciting work God is doing. The Johnsons and their neighbors are excited to see their children being discipled, learning what it means to be and live like Jesus.

Imagine what would happen if we had communities of Jesus followers like this in every neighborhood and in every city in our country and around the world! I believe we'd see the kind of revival that occurred in the early church — the fulfillment of Acts 1:8 all over again. If you are excited by this vision, let me ask you a question: After reading all this, are you *in*? If the answer is yes, then let me encourage you to get started. Do what the Johnsons did. Devoting yourself to much prayer and discussion, take out a sheet of paper and map out a plan. Read the story of the first church in the book of Acts, and prepare to be amazed as God does what only God can do.

Part 4

IMPLEMENTING A CONNECTING CHURCH

Chapter 12

MISTAKES I'VE MADE ...
LESSONS I'VE LEARNED

In this new section in *The Connecting Church*, I speak primarily to leaders in churches who may want to implement a connecting church vision. But first, I need to say that over the past ten years since *The Connecting Church* was published, I've come to realize that I made some mistakes. But I think mistakes are inevitable. Here's why.

I've come to terms with the fact that there is no way a person can venture into new territory and calculate everything perfectly. If you wait until you are completely confident and have all your ducks in a row, you will never act. The late and astoundingly wise Peter Drucker writes, "The future requires decisions — now. It imposes risk — now. It requires action — now. It demands allocation of resources, and above all, of human resources — now. It requires work — now."[1]

So when I first sensed the call of God and did what the Johnsons did, taking the leap and going "all in," I naturally made some mistakes. But I've also found comfort in these words from Drucker: "The first time around, a new strategy very often doesn't work. Then one must sit down and ask what has been learned ... Try to improve it, to change it, and make another major effort."[2] A retired general who was active in our congregation in San Antonio taught me, "Every plan works until the first shot is fired!"

So yes, ten years ago I acted on a God-given dream with a

plan, and I made some mistakes. I overlooked and underestimated some things. But I've learned from my mistakes, recognizing several things I didn't get at the time. Today, I'm trying to humbly rework the plan and make another major effort to live out the vision presented in this book. To be clear, not everything I share in the chapters that follow is the result of what I've learned from my failures and mistakes. Some is new simply because we've gone through several rapid changes in our society. Today, with developments in technology, the growth of the Internet, and shifts in the economy, society changes quickly. A decision made in the morning may seem antiquated by the end of the day.

Still, I've learned some lessons from ten years of implementing the connecting church vision, and I'll now share my top ten with you.

1. Realize that biblical community is a way of life, not a program. Above everything else, I want to emphasize that biblical community is a way of life, not a program to be implemented by a church staff. This is by far the granddaddy realization of them all. If you try to implement the connecting church vision without adequate commitment and a community of people who are willing to embrace change and carry out experiments, this will be seen as just another addition to the already overbooked schedules of busy people. And I can guarantee it will fail.

Our family had a two- to three-year jump on making changes in our life before we introduced it to our congregation in Fort Worth. We didn't realize at the time how important this was — that we had had time to test, fail, learn, and develop habits before daring to share this vision with our church.

When it dawned on us that we needed to capture people with vision before trying to implement a program, I began to teach these concepts in our membership classes. These classes ultimately led me to write a book with my wife called *Making Room for Life*.[3] Now expanded under the title *Real Simplicity*, the book seeks to lay out the principles of this way of life and offer a compelling vision that captures the heart.[4] To anyone seeking to implement a vision for biblical community in a church today, I encourage you to begin by casting the vision, capturing the heart, and then talking about the new way of community life we present here in *The Connecting Church.*

In other words, leader, step one begins with you and your family. To pass it on to others, you must be able to model it in your own life. Then let me suggest that if you intend to implement the connecting church vision in your church, you build into your plan a vision-casting phase of one to two years during which you teach people this paradigm as a way of life.

2. Teach a theology of biblical community. People need to be given a chance to see the rich theology and vision of God that drives this movement. We need to give people a glimpse of the nature of God as a community of loving persons. We need to emphasize the social aspects of our creation in the image of God, not just the psychological, individualistic viewpoint most of us have grown up on (i.e., that we are made up individually of body, soul, and spirit). We need to expose people to the rich theology of place—the fact that location matters and gives context and nuance to our understanding of God and one another. We need to show people that they have been hardwired for community and that if they deprive themselves of community, it will kill them, both emotionally and physically.

This is no easy task. I realize this vision is undoubtedly different from what you've been taught. Most of the people in the American church have grown up eating, drinking, and breathing individualism. They naturally read the Bible through the eyes of an individualist. For example, when they read Ephesians 6:10 – 17, where Paul highlights the importance of the armor of God, they think about how it applies to their lives as individuals. Rarely do they stop to think about the context in which Paul is writing— that he is speaking to a *community* of Christians and addressing how to make community work with people of diverse and often hostile backgrounds (think Jews and Gentiles).

Once they begin to recognize the biblical emphasis on

community and the way it informs their reading and understanding of the Scriptures, they will likely sense a growing excitement. Once they've tasted these truths, they can't go back. I can confess I've been "wrecked" forever! We need congregations filled with folks who see what we see and are willing to try something different, something new and countercultural. It all begins by seeing and understanding the biblical vision.

3. Realize that success requires a connector. In his national bestseller *The Tipping Point*, Malcolm Gladwell popularized the term "Connector" to refer to people with a special gift for bringing the world together.[5] Gladwell goes on to say that these people are "sprinkled among every walk of life ... are a handful of people with a truly extraordinary knack of making friends and acquaintances."[6] It's easy to see connectors in the New Testament and the early church. Every time I read about Aquila and Priscilla, it seems like they are hosting a party. The church meets at their house, no matter what city they live in.[7] Connectors are the people who draw the group together, initiate the meetings, and facilitate the gatherings that lead to community formation.

As I look at the successful and sustainable neighborhood groups we've started over the last eighteen years, they have all had a leader with this connector magnetism. And without a connector, a group is sure to fail. The person doesn't necessarily have to be a genuine, certifiable "Connector," as Gladwell describes it, but they are often a friendly person who has both relational intelligence and a love for other people. With these simple gifts, a person can help create a vibrant community in a small neighborhood. Gladwell suggests that "while most of us are busily choosing whom we would like to know, and rejecting the people who don't look right ... [Connectors] like them all.[8] This is the mindset that is needed to form a healthy, biblical community.

One of the best compliments my wife, Rozanne, and I have received over the last twenty years is that we are connectors. People will tell me that the connecting church vision works for us so well *because* we are wired to initiate relationships. While I'll admit this is true, I don't believe this means the vision we are talking about needs to be limited to certain personality types. We should note that *every* author in the New Testament letters includes a call for people to show hospitality. In other words, let's recognize the strategic value in finding connectors, people naturally gifted in this area, but let's not use the fact that some are wired to bring people together as an excuse to neglect the call to live in community.

Lay out the challenge and trust that the Spirit will ignite the presence of Christ in the neighborhood. We need to remind people of 1 Corinthians 12 — that while it may take a connector gift to bring folks together, it takes all of the gifts to pull off the mission once the folks come together and go out to serve.

4. Give this vision a try. I can't tell you how many times over the last twenty years I've heard someone tell me, "But I don't even *like* my neighbors! If they are Christians, it takes everything inside of me not to arrange an immediate meeting with their maker!" The mistake I made early on was to simply agree and admit it wouldn't work. "Oh, well," I'd say. "I guess you're off the hook and this just won't work for you. I'm sorry you live in such a rotten neighborhood with people like that." Of course, I didn't actually say that. But I wasn't sure how to respond, so I admitted that for some neighborhoods, the connecting church vision just might not work.

I've come to realize there is a deeper problem behind this objection. Often, it isn't that people don't *like* their neighbors; it's that they don't actually *know* their neighbors. But we have more in common with our neighbors than we realize. In the suburbs, most neighborhoods are segregated by price, which means your neighbors are likely to be in the same economic class as you. In addition, if you own your home, you share in common the desire to protect one of your largest investments. Your children likely go to the same school, and you likely shop at the same grocery store.

Auren Hoffman, an American entrepreneur, believes that if you find someone boring, it is only because you, the listener, haven't asked the right questions or found that person's true passions.[9] This matches my own experience. Getting to know a new person is better than watching a documentary, reality television, or a sitcom any day of the week. Get a little curious and learn to ask the right questions. Your neighbors may not be as bad as you think. In fact, you may even start to like them.

I am convinced that once you experience the power of *proximity* in your relationships, you will be hooked on becoming friends with your neighbors. The experience of popping in and out for short visits will quickly become a new, life-giving experience for you.

One initiative we've built into the launch of new neighborhood gatherings is to pull people who live in the same neighborhood together for a dessert and then invite them to try six monthly gatherings to learn more about the concept. Why six months? Six to seven months seems to be the amount of time it takes for people to connect and to start getting to know each other. At the end of the six-month experience, we ask if they would like to continue on or break up. Most continue on. Why? Once they hear their neighbors' stories and discover how interesting they are, they realize just how much they have in common.

5. Realize that the vision takes five to seven years to fully implement. Another lesson I've learned is that the transition time for an existing church to become a connecting church is much longer than I anticipated. And the transition is much harder than living out the actual vision you desire in the end. That's not to say it isn't enjoyable. Gathering on Sundays for worship and then spending the remaining six days centered on your neighborhood and local community is a pleasurable, life-giving experience. But when I first started this journey at Pantego Bible Church in 1994, I had no idea it would take so long for the connecting church concept to become fully operational and to gain traction in the culture of the church. As I look back, I realize it took at least seven years for the idea to gain the strength to stand up on its own. It was a painful experience, and I vowed never to do it again.

But I've also learned not to make vows I can't keep. Since leaving Pantego Bible Church, I have journeyed to Chicago and now to

San Antonio to help two other churches, at their request, make the transition to a more biblical experience of community life. In each case, I've let them know up front that embarking on this journey is a commitment of at least five to seven years of hard, sometimes painful work. I've let them know that attendance might drop. I've even put some of this in writing in an "official" ministry plan. Knowing what to expect brings some comfort to the people and particularly to the leaders. It helps to set realistic expectations and avoid the "quick fix" syndrome that is all too common today.

Unfortunately, in both places where I served, the leadership quickly forgot the time commitment involved, and after encountering the first serious obstacle, they were ready to abandon ship. So how do you guarantee you'll continue past this point? I love what Hernán Cortés is said to have done when his band of explorers landed on the shores of Mexico to start a new way of life—a life Cortés knew would be difficult. He burned the ships so his men would understand there could be no turning back. Am I suggesting that you burn down the church building? No, of course not! I'm afraid that what made Cortés an inspirational leader would land me in jail as an arsonist. But one thing that can help is to make sure the leadership is "all in" from the beginning. As you take steps to show them that the cost of moving back to old patterns is more costly than continuing forward, you are likely to stay the course.

6. Include people from other churches. When our family moved into our second neighborhood in Arlington, Texas, we were armed with ideas and intentionality for reaching this little neighborhood of one hundred homes. We began with a group of five families that attended Pantego Bible Church. As time went on, families that attended other churches also began coming to our weekly home group gathering. I thought it was very cool that members of other churches would get involved. But I didn't expect these families to soon transfer their membership to Pantego.

Not long after this happened, a rumor spread through the neighborhood gossip mill that we were using these gatherings as a ploy to gain more members for our church. Ouch! I certainly desired and anticipated that our church would grow, but I never envisioned our gatherings as a way to steal members from other churches. Fortunately, two families that joined the group were quite satisfied with their local Vineyard church. Their inclusion and involvement in the group gave evidence we weren't invested in stealing members.

It's important to include believers from different churches for at least two reasons. First, it's a great way to visibly demonstrate the *unity* of the body of Christ and show the world how the universal church works together. In neighborhood ministry, there is little need to squabble over church doctrine or the "proper" way to be baptized or take Communion. Our challenges are focused on the lonely widow across the street who needs a hug or the single mom who needs the leaves removed from her gutters. We have discovered that Calvinists and Armenians, Catholics and Protestants, and immersionists and sprinklers can all work together to accomplish neighborhood community. One of the reasons nonchurched people stay away from the church and from God is that they see the fighting along denominational lines. When the unbelieving world sees the church united around local causes, it softens their hearts toward the gospel.

A second reason is related to *density*. A common objection from people is that there isn't anyone from the church who lives in their neighborhood. The farther away you get from the church building, the less likely you are to encounter families from your church. It's harder for people to form a Christian hub within their neighborhood if the pool of participants is limited to those who attend a single church. When you give permission for your people to join with believers who attend other churches, they are more likely to find at least two to three other households willing to join them. If you don't give permission, then you must necessarily draw bigger geographical circles to encompass what defines a "neighborhood." But I don't recommend it. Here's why.

7. Keep this equation in mind when implementing the connecting church vision: shrink circle + raise ownership

= **increased impact.** The smaller the circle you use to define a "neighborhood," the better. In his practical guide to forming neighborhood community groups titled *The Great Neighborhood Book*, Jay Walljasper writes, "When it comes to neighborhoods, like so many human institutions, small is definitely beautiful. It's hard to foster a sense of community or get things done in an area that encompasses too much space or includes too many people."[10] So what is that ideal size for defining a neighborhood? Architectural theorist Christopher Alexander recommends neighborhoods be defined as "not more than 300 yards across with no more than 400–500 inhabitants ... Keep major roads outside these neighborhoods."[11] This is a helpful rule of thumb.

Again, why is smaller better? Here's a simple analogy to consider: Take two spoonfuls of a concentrated power drink. If you throw that powder in a bucket of water, it will not be as potent as it will be if you pour it into an eight-ounce glass. In the same way, a small band of Christians coming together to be the presence of Christ in their neighborhood has a more powerful, concentrated effect. Pour this group of believers into a small neighborhood, and the taste of Christ will be much stronger.

In addition to shrinking the circle geographically, it's wise to try to increase the sense of ownership among the members of your group. Walljasper writes:

> Long experience has shown us that bottom-up strategies work better than top-down approaches. The bottom-up strategy recognizes citizens as the experts, is guided by the wisdom of the community, and builds a strong partnership between the public and private sectors. This is the most important thing we've learned in the more than 30 years we've been working to make great neighborhoods.[12]

David Bornstein agrees. He is a journalist who has written about powerful grassroots movements such as the Grameen Bank's micro-loans to the poor in Bangladesh. He concludes that "well-funded efforts, with clear outcomes, that spell out the steps to get there do not work. Changes that begin on a large scale, are initiated or imposed from the top, and are driven to produce quick wins inevitably produce few lasting results ... This means that sustainable changes in community occur locally on a small scale, happen slowly, and are initiated at a grassroots level."[13]

When I first started growing Christian communities in neighborhoods, I plotted every move down to the smallest details. I now realize this limited the sense of ownership that is naturally created when you give folks the opportunity to decide for themselves what needs to be done and at what frequency. Those who live in a neighborhood typically know best what needs to be done. When people create and own an idea, they will fight for it and put their own time and energy into it more than they will simply adopt an idea that came from command control.

8. Don't use all of your time margin on yourself and other Christians. A lack of time margin remains one of the greatest obstacles to growing Christian community in America (or any of the other exceptionally busy, purchase-hungry, fragmented places in the world). People typically have little time margin to play with, particularly at the beginning of this journey. As they embrace this connecting church vision as a way of life, more time will be freed up as they opt for less time in the car and spend more time in their neighborhood. In the beginning, leaders need to coach people on how to use their limited time.

When I began this journey, I simply transferred my ideas of a traditional, church-based small group into our neighborhood community group. We strongly encouraged our new groups to meet weekly *in addition* to attending weekly worship services at the church building. This helped to expedite a sense of belonging among our congregants, which increased the frequency of contact and helped people feel at home in the church more quickly. On the front end of the journey this made sense. We found, however, that if the group is not careful, they will use all of their time and energy meeting with each other, with little time left for other, non-Christian neighbors. That approach doesn't seem to match the mission of the church, does it?

Over the years, I've shifted my thinking on this matter. We now suggest that Christians in a neighborhood gather for an "official" planned meeting about once a month. At this gathering, they share a meal together, read Scripture, pray, and, most important, talk about their intentional plans for "being Jesus" in the neighborhood. Ideally this frees up time for them to gather throughout the month in more organic ways—joining other neighbors for dinner, attending a neighborhood-sponsored event, starting a Bible study, helping a widow with her yard work ... the list of possibilities are only limited by the willingness and creativity of the group.

Another successful church that has embraced the neighborhood model of community encourages their groups to meet weekly during the school year (September through May) and then take time off in the summer to hang with neighbors in more intentional ways. Whatever your plan when it comes to scheduling time together, be careful to avoid "holy huddles," where you fail to seize opportunities to be with the people in your neighborhood who are outside your small group.

9. Evaluate the good and bad of the multisite church model. The latest trend to sweep the church over the last ten years has been the multisite church movement—one church having multiple services spread out over multiple locations. When I was at Willow Creek Community Church in the Chicago suburbs, we had four campuses. At Oak Hills Church in San Antonio, where I currently serve on staff, we have five campuses.

Churches decide to adopt the multisite model for a variety of reasons, but one reason especially attracted me to the concept. I had a vision for Oak Hills to have enough campuses around our city so anyone who wanted to be involved with what God was doing through us could reach a campus on Sunday morning in less than twenty minutes' drive from where they lived. Not only would this cut down on the commute for our parishioners, but it would also make inviting their neighbors to the physical church building more palatable. In other words, for a growing, expanding church, the multisite model helps overcome some of the problems associated with people commuting to church gatherings located far from their neighborhood. In the next chapter, we'll look at a paradigm for reaching a city. I call it the spider model, and it covers this approach in more detail.

If a church is serious about reaching neighborhoods in a city, I recommend holding off on the start of a new campus until there are *already* a host of small neighborhood gatherings up and running in that area. Why? One of the downsides to multisite campuses is that it takes energy and margin — commitment from people that requires time and resources. When launching a new campus, the initiating leadership typically uses all of its energy and margin to pull off the worship services and children's/student ministries at the campus and there will be nothing left for investment back into the community. With limited resources and time, believers will be inclined to huddle together at the building.

Initially, we thought that launching a new multisite campus would foster further growth in neighborhoods and avoid the inherent problems of a centralized main campus. This hasn't been the case. Now we opt to postpone the opening of new campuses until we have a sufficient number of grassroots neighborhood groups in an area to support it.

10. Realize that people learn and get information differently. Rapid, reliable, and increased innovation in technology is changing the game. Let me give you an example. Recently, our daughter and son-in-law introduced us to Roku. Perhaps you have Apple TV, and maybe by the time this book comes out, this technology will have been replaced by something new. But here's the basic idea. We have a little box (or a USB drive that plugs into the TV) that connects with our home Wi-Fi and eliminates costly monthly bills to a cable or satellite network company. We go to the channel store and simply choose the channels we're interested in having. Most are free. Our favorite is Netflix, which costs us a few dollars a month. We gain access to movies and television series with no commercials. No taping or deleting from the box is necessary, and we stop and start whenever we want to. We don't even have to remember which episode we watched last. When is the next episode on? Whenever we choose. We can even take our little box with us on a vacation at the beach.

This has certainly gotten me wondering: How does this affect the way we disperse information, teach, and engage in discipleship? Oak Hills was one of the first churches to offer a channel on Roku. It's free, and it has every sermon series Max Lucado and I have taught since I arrived in San Antonio. Just as you can with a television series, you can pick a sermon series and watch each message in HD, whenever you want to, anywhere you want to. We have over nine thousand subscribers from around the world!

In the first edition of *The Connecting Church*, I assumed the primary way for people to engage in the study of Scripture was the sermon. If you missed it, you missed it. But now, it is possible to watch sermons online after the fact or even to live stream a message from anywhere in the world (from your phone!). These changes in technology open up new avenues for the church and for the way we conceive of community gatherings—the way groups of Christians gathering together in community relate to one another across a city, in the same geographic region, and around the world. See chapter 16 for more about this.

■ ■

These are just some of the mistakes I've made and new insights I've had over the past ten years. Let me end where I began: There is no way a person can journey into new territory and calculate everything perfectly. If you wait until you have all your ducks in a row, you will never do anything. My advice to you? Learn from the experiences and mistakes of others so you can avoid unnecessary pitfalls. But don't wait to act. In ten years, you can write a book about the things you've learned, and I promise you that I'll read it. Deal?

Chapter 13

CHOOSING A PATH

In 2007, a friend recommended a book that provides visual ways of understanding some of my concerns with the process of implementing the connecting church vision. It puts words to some of my doubts and frustrations. The book, *The Starfish and the Spider*, identifies two types of organizations—spider organizations and starfish organizations.[1]

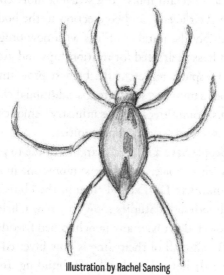

Illustration by Rachel Sansing

THE SPIDER CHURCH

A spider organization has a head, a body, numerous legs, and a web that catches bugs. This type of organization has a top-down structure, and it usually has a CEO, a president, and a number of vice presidents. Applying this model to today's typical church, the head represents a senior pastor, the body the building of the organization, and the legs various church programs and the specialized staff needed to run them.

The goal of the church is simple: to attract as many people as possible to the web woven by the spider and get them stuck in the web. The spider church achieves this by means of the Sunday morning service and its supporting children's programs. Everything ultimately leads up to the thirty-minute sermon given by the pastor. Sitting in a room together on Sunday morning is fundamentally what it means to "go to church."

If a spider church successfully attracts people, it grows. And the bigger it gets, the less connected the people tend to feel. So what do you do to retain folks? You weave a more complicated web to deepen their loyalty and connection to the body and the head. You multiply the number of legs with new programs that help people address their need for relationships and growth. The eight legs of the spider represent the biggest programs — men's ministry, women's ministry, small groups, additional children and youth programs, committees, singles ministry, senior citizen Sunday school classes, and serving opportunities.

Because people have a limited margin of time to invest, they will be faced with a choice: "Do I invest more time in the church or in the community? Do I spend time in the church building or in my neighborhood?" Studies show that new Christians who join a church often don't have any nonchurched friends after two years. Why? Because all of their time is now invested in church programs typically housed in the church building. In suburbia, the church is a silo separated from the rest of the broader community — a subculture, if you will.

Typically, the people who demonstrate the strongest level of commitment to the church are the people who are *least connected* in the community-at-large. They are satisfied with the church and become the leaders and power brokers in that church. They enjoy the church because their need for community is met by the frequent encounters they have with others in their church programs. Their whole life may be wrapped up in the church, its building, and its programs.

I have been the senior pastor or teaching pastor of several large spider churches for over twenty years now, and I can tell you firsthand that significant life change often occurs with this method of church. I've seen people come to Christ, families restored, folks healed of addictions, faith in God deepened, and the Word faithfully taught.

But the problem is that the spider church model doesn't fit well with the overall vision I share in this book. Why? Because the basic architecture of the organization prohibits a number of things from happening. To accomplish the connecting church vision, the structure must change. It must shift from being a spider church to a starfish church.

THE STARFISH CHURCH

A starfish has five fingers that join together. The center of the starfish body is not like the head of a spider. It's not a brain or command control center. Rather, each finger of the starfish contains the whole idea of what it means to be a starfish. Brafman and Beckstrom call this the ultimate decentralized organization.

Illustration by Rachel Sansing

The community the Johnsons created with others in their small neighborhood isn't a centralized organization. They fellowship, study the Bible, disciple their children, care for each other, hold each other accountable, give money, use their spiritual gifts, serve the widow and orphans in their neighborhood and community, help the poor, and even engage personally in supporting ministries internationally. They may take Communion during their mealtime as a group and even baptize in a neighbor's pool those who trust Christ.

On my journey over the last two decades, I've come to see that Jesus' vision for the church is more like a starfish construct than a spider one. It was never God's perfect will for his presence to be placed in a box. Even in the construction of the ultimate "God box" — the Old Testament temple — God gave his people an indication that centralized, man-made structures were not the end goal for the gathering of his people. God had his message sent to David through the prophet Nathan after David expressed his desire to build God a beautiful temple:

> "Are you the one to build me a house to dwell in? I have not dwelt in a house from the day I brought the Israelites up out of Egypt to this day. I have been moving from place to place with a tent as my dwelling. Wherever I have moved with all the Israelites, did I ever say to any of their rulers whom I commanded to shepherd my people Israel, 'Why have you not built me a house of cedar?' "[2]

In other words, God liked the idea of being on the move. Whenever he wanted to work, he revealed himself in the time and place he desired. He could appear in the form of a cloud by day or a fire by night, and when the people saw God leading them, they took down the tent and followed. And though God did allow the temple to be built, it was clear this arrangement was only temporary. When Jesus breathed his last breath on the cross and sins were fully paid for, the curtain in the temple that separated God from the people was torn from top to bottom.[3] Years later, the temple building itself would be destroyed. Did this mean God was no longer present with his people?

No. After the crucifixion, the visible presence of God — the place where he chose to manifest himself on earth — was transferred from the temple building to the followers of Jesus — the *new* temple, not made of stones but of transformed hearts.[4] The church we read about in Acts 2:42 – 47 is not a church building; it's a community that meets in a home around a dinner table. God's presence indwells each believer, and when they gather together, Jesus' presence is palpably present in their gatherings.[5] The activities we read about in the book of Acts are not "programs" run by a centralized organization (e.g., the belonging program, the growing program, the serving program); they are the experience of those who gather together. Historians estimate there were about thirty people in each house church. If that is true, then there were around a hundred house gatherings honeycombed throughout the city of Jerusalem immediately following Peter's sermon (which was given in the town square, not a church building).[6] Each house gathering represented a finger of the starfish, each containing within it the whole idea of the church.

I have experienced this principle at work in the four neighborhoods we've lived in for the past twenty-five years. When we moved into our current neighborhood several years ago, we didn't know a single soul. After a year, we began a faith-based monthly neighborhood gathering (similar to what I describe in chapter 11) with a handful of Christian neighbors we had met from different churches. As I shared earlier, as of this writing, 58 of the 150 households in the neighborhood are still connected to our gathering — nearly 40 percent of our entire neighborhood. Can you imagine the challenges a spider church would face in reaching 40 percent of its community? In our city, that percentage would represent about 577,500 people and would require several rather large buildings with multiple sites and lots of staff. The starfish church model, on the other hand, keeps things very simple. It uses the real estate of its members and costs next to nothing!

Each month, somewhere around thirty to fifty people gather in our home and in several other homes in our neighborhood to share a meal, read the Word, pray, and decide how God wants to use us during the next thirty days to be his hands and his feet to those around us. During the week, we have two women's Bible studies that include mothers and some of their daughters. We have two men's discipleship groups taking a chronological journey through an edition of the Bible called *The Story*, and each man has made a commitment to take someone else through the study at the same time.[7] The men with children at home lead their families through the experience. One of our empty nesters is taking four inmates through a study in a prison. On Saturday, the women meet as a prayer group.

We have a responsive care system within our neighborhood as well. Families with new babies get meals; a woman who lost her husband is visited and listened to; a dad in a severe car accident has all his house projects done by the men of the group as he recovers. We organized a 5K Fun Run to provide food for a dynamic local organization that helps the poor; one hundred people from our neighborhood participated in it. Several of us pair up to mentor families and children at risk through this ministry. We sponsored a National Night Out with a huge turnout in three locations in our neighborhood.[8]

You get the idea. Even more than the list of gatherings and activities, the encounters in the "spaces in between" excite me most—seeing each other while taking out the trash, leaving for work, going out for a jog, or walking the dog. Smaller, more intimate dinners are planned at the last minute. Phone calls are made just to check in. Of course, e-mails, evites, tweets, and texts are rampant among us, but these are still secondary to actually gathering together. All of this is to say that our little neighborhood group carries on much of the day-to-day work the church is meant to do. Our location is not a church building; it's a neighborhood.

So then, you might be asking, "What is the problem?" Well, ask yourself if what I've just described and the vision spelled out in this book match your own experience in the church. If not, how in the world will these two ways of doing and being the church fit together? Let me put it this way: What do you get when you mate a spider with a starfish? You don't know? Neither do I. That's where all of this gets really hard. There are no easy answers, no quick fixes for figuring this out.

WHERE DO WE GO FROM HERE?

In today's church, we see two paradigms — two legitimate and effective models of ministry to accomplish God's vision for the church. One movement is led by the spider church. In this model, masterful leaders of the change process must follow the leading of the Spirit and empower and equip large numbers of people to head out of the building and ignite the presence of Christ through small communities in every neighborhood in their city. In chapter 14, I'll share my best ideas on how this can be done within the existing framework of a spider church. I will summarize some of how we're currently implementing this at Oak Hills, as well as tell a little bit about what's happening in a few other, highly successful churches.

We cannot simply ignore the spider model. It remains attractive to a large majority of churchgoers. Some folks know of no other experience and find comfort in the familiar. With good leadership at work, many of the people sitting in pews and theater seats today can make the shift to embrace a vision for neighborhood-based, biblical community. In their hearts, most people long for this deep experience of community and truly want to be a part of a church that reaches out and takes seriously Jesus' command to love our neighbor. Due to structural limitations, their efforts will often not be as potent as those who utilize the starfish model, but through sheer numbers they will make an impact in their local communities.

The starfish church will lead the second movement. Who will be attracted to this movement? I believe it will be two growing groups of people. First, many of those in the Millennial generation, people who came of age at the beginning of the twenty-first century, will be leaders in this movement. Studies show that many in this group of young adults are leaving the church *building* when they leave the nest and have no plans to return. Not all, however, are abandoning their *faith* in Jesus Christ. They are just not interested in the traditional, organized churches that meet in buildings. Their experience of community is often shaped by different factors from the ones that shaped previous generations. Technology has changed the way they learn and relate to others. Their connection points are more spontaneous and organic, and are even smaller. They have a different concept of mission. While the Gen Xers reacted intellectually to the materialism of the Baby Boomer generation, Millennials seem more interested in *doing* something. With its decentralized, fluid conception of church, the starfish model appeals to them.

But I also regularly meet older folks, often empty nesters, who have logged their hours in a church building, raised their children in them, and faithfully given their tithes, but have simply lost their steam for another capital campaign due to the cost, complexity, and passivity promoted by top-down models of church. These are mature believers who have a huge passion for Christ's mission and want to make a difference with the time they have left. I have met dozens of them over the last few years, and they are serious leaders with much to offer if only they can be unleashed. They usually share their thoughts in secret, quiet gathering places at night, almost like Nicodemus did when he sought to have a vulnerable conversation with Jesus. They feel guilty, but at the same time they feel something passionate stirring within them. When they see this new, yet ancient, expression of the church emerging, they want to be among the early adopters.

THE COMMON CAUSE

While the spider model excels at attracting and gathering large numbers of people together and the starfish model is highly effective in reproducing groups of Jesus followers in community, there is one thing these two designs hold in common: they both want to see people grow into the image of Christ and follow the lead of God's Spirit to serve others in love. This is, and in my estimation has always been, the heart of the Christian revolution. Fancy sermons do not hold a candle to the flames of Christian community as it enfolds people, teaches them what it means to follow Christ, and sends them out in the power of the Spirit. As Francis Schaeffer once wrote, "The final apologetic which Jesus gives is the observable love of true Christians for true Christians."[9]

The challenge for the spider church in America today is helping people learn to exit the building and reclaim the neighborhood—helping to form Christian community where people live and work each day. This is what we desperately need to see. It will take both spider and starfish churches focused on this cause to counter the pull of our individualistic, isolated, consumerist culture. The church of the twenty-first century must embrace the mission best expressed in the simple children's song we teach in Sunday school:

> This little light of mine, I'm gonna let it shine.
> This little light of mine, I'm gonna let it shine.
> This little light of mine, I'm gonna let it shine.
> Let it shine, let it shine, let it shine!
>
> Hide it under a bushel—No! I'm gonna let it shine ...
>
> [Hide it under a *building*—No! I'm gonna let it shine ...]
>
> All around the neighborhood, I'm gonna let it shine.
> All around the neighborhood, I'm gonna let it shine.
> All around the neighborhood, I'm gonna let it shine.
> Let it shine, let it shine, let it shine!

Chapter 14
IMPLEMENTING A HYBRID VISION

This chapter is for those who lead or serve in a church that meets in a building and has a pastor, rector, or priest, as well as staff members and programs. In the last chapter, I referred to this structure as the spider church. And while I think our culture is increasingly interested in alternative structures for church, I don't see things changing soon. The spider paradigm is still the primary model in America today and will continue to be for the foreseeable future.

If you are interested in the connecting church vision of moving your people out of the building during the week to form smaller communities in the neighborhoods they live in, then this chapter will give you ideas to do just that. Adopting this vision entails moving to a structure that is something of a hybrid of the starfish and the spider. While you will still have a central leader, building, and worship service, you will also need to find ways to effectively mobilize your congregation to participate in *decentralized* experiences in their neighborhoods so that the people will learn to take greater ownership and begin to *be* the church rather than just *going to* church. The bad news is that transitions are never easy; the good news is that it can be done (and has been done) with amazing kingdom outcomes.

TWO ENVIRONMENTS

Two environments make up the hybrid model: the campus environment and the neighborhood environment.

Campus Environment	Neighborhood Environment
church building	several homes in a neighborhood

Each of these environments has a distinct purpose that complements the purpose of the other one.

The Campus Environment

In this hybrid model, several activities continue to take place at a centralized church building, including worship services and children's and student ministries. In addition, as a church grows, special opportunities may arise for using a building to serve needs in the community.

Worship

Along with expressing what is unique to your denomination or church tradition, it is important that your worship service gathering times include opportunities to inspire and train your people for missional living in their community. Instead of the concept that six days lead up to the Sunday service, think about how the Sunday service serves as the catalyst for the other six days. The heart of the gathering is no longer digesting a message on one day; the heart is equipping people to be the church for the other six days of the week. The service gathering seeks to point people to God, the cross, and the mission God is calling them to embrace and live. It calls people to join in the story of God.

Use the worship service to tell stories of how people in the congregation are being used as God's hands and feet out in the neighborhoods and communities through the power of the Holy Spirit within them. Use this time to offer prayers of hope and healing. Finally, dismiss your people with a benediction to go out to *be* the church in God's strength. Here is the benediction I give at the end of each service:

> Now go out into the world in peace.
> Have courage.
> Hold on to what is good.
> Honor all people.
> Strengthen the fainthearted.
> Support the weak.
> Help the suffering and share the gospel.
> Love and serve the Lord in the power of the Holy Spirit.
> And may the grace of our Lord Jesus Christ be with you all.
> Amen.[1]

Children's Ministry

One of the key drivers in many churches is a centralized children's program. Christian families may feel inadequate to be the principal drivers of their children's spiritual development and desire the assistance of a professional children's Bible program. One of the keys to your numerical success at the building will be the real and perceived quality of this program in your community. The church with the best children's program on Sunday morning is often the best attended in town.

The principal objective of the children's program (birth to fifth grade) is to effectively teach the stories of the Bible in a safe, fun, clean, and nurturing environment. Several good curriculums are available to achieve this purpose, but I suggest looking for one that includes parental involvement. Participation by parents in the spiritual development of their children is the biggest predictor of the continuation of children's faith once they leave the nest.

One option is the vast array of resources surrounding *The*

Story, developed by our church and published by Zondervan. The curriculums for adult, youth, and children's ministries, based on an abridged chronology of the Bible, take you through the school year, enabling children, teens, and adults to study the same story each week. Having everyone on the same story greatly aids parents who have more than one child. Each child has their own copy of *The Story* appropriate for their age, and teachers have curriculum for each age group, along with suggestions for how the parents can get involved at home.[2]

Student Ministry

Student ministry is equally important for the centralized campus environment. When teens are in a home, parents often allow them to choose the church their family will attend. This, in my estimation, will go down in American history as one of the tragic patterns of Christian parenting. It's still a reality we must learn to live with, however — at least for now. At the very least, it means that churches must seek to have an effective and compelling student ministry. Here are three workable ideas for engaging students.

1. Encourage teens to attend worship with their parents and hold a student gathering on a different night of the week. If the family can stay an additional hour, encourage them to serve together in children's ministry or another volunteer role. Also encourage older students to disciple younger students before, during, or after school.

2. Have a teen worship service at the same time as the main service and allow parents and others to attend. Hold a gathering for students on another evening of the week for small discipleship groups. If your church draws from multiple high schools, encourage gatherings of students in someone's home located near the school.

3. Conduct a student service during a particular time and then encourage the students to attend the main service with their parents during the second hour.

Students who have received a solid understanding of the stories of the Bible through their children's ministry experience or from their parents will still need additional building blocks before they leave home so that, with God's help, they can stand on a foundation of faith. These blocks include:

1. Knowing how to study and engage the Bible for themselves. This is a huge problem within the ranks of Christianity. While we can (and will likely have to) spoon-feed students with slick, media-wowing presentations to retain them or their parents, we must help them gain the necessary skills for accessing the Scriptures for themselves before they leave home.[3]

2. Gaining functional competence on the big ideas of Christianity. Students must be schooled in the common creeds of the Christian faith to develop a worldview that helps them see and evaluate their life experiences. They don't need to be scholars, but they should be "functionally competent," knowing enough so they can apply the truth to daily life. They should grasp certain core beliefs, core practices, and core virtues of biblical Christianity. See the appendix for my list of the thirty biggest ideas of the Bible.

3. Having a personal growth plan. Before students leave home, they must shift from getting into the Bible to letting the Bible get into them. Instead of just studying the life of Jesus, they must begin the long journey of actually becoming like Jesus. Students who have been given a solid foundation in the Bible now require a personal, customized spiritual growth plan that comes out of personal and communal evaluation and leads them to "best practices" resources for ongoing, dynamic spiritual growth.[4]

Of course, children and students need more than knowledge and plans; they need a community that nurtures, inspires, models, challenges, and develops them. While the centralized children's and student ministries of the church are helpful tools to encourage our younger generations, the neighborhood environment will be the primary community that surrounds them and their family.

Special Growth Needs

A number of years ago, psychologist and author Larry Crabb made a stunning announcement in which he suggested that many of the problems that humans deal with are not psychological in nature but "soul cries" that can be cared for in a loving, healthy community of laypeople.[5] I remember reading those words and jumping for joy. Others, however, doubted the truth of what he stated. But the Bible I read suggests that Crabb's theory is accurate. The problem is that the individualism of our culture makes it difficult to sustain the type of community that functions in a healthy way.

But even if we assume that the people in our hybrid model of church are engaged in healthy, biblical community, what about the genuine psychological problems people face? Crabb believes certain issues and struggles will always require the assistance of a specialist. In other words, the church will still need qualified counselors, trained theologians, and special programs that help people break through struggles, answer complex questions that arise, and meet needs that cannot be met in lay community experience. These are the types of "special" programs that are appropriate to sponsor at a church building, ideally on a weeknight. In this sense, the church becomes an equipping center, a location for receiving specialized training.

If you can just rent a space to use one day a week, do it. Only pay for what you use. The goal in the connecting church model is to convene community gatherings in the neighborhoods. If you already own a building and have access to it 24/7, however, then it is wise to be a good steward of it. Consider inviting community organizations to use it for their needs — Boy Scouts, Girl Scouts, dance classes, civic meetings, concerts, graduations, and so on. In some cases, it may be appropriate to charge them, either to recoup basic maintenance costs or even to make a small profit to offset the cost of other ministry initiatives. In many cases, you can offer the building for free as a service to your community to build goodwill and to tear down the silos that exist among religious, business, educational, nonprofit, and civic life. A neighborhood-based church in Peoria, Arizona—Christ's Church of the Valley—offers its building free of charge for any person in the community as the setting for a funeral service for a loved one. This is spot-on and goes a long way to enjoy the favor of the people in your community.[6]

The Neighborhood Environment

The second environment to consider is the local *neighborhood*. Here you are seeking to create small circles of believers who live in the same geographic area and are seeking to ignite the presence of Christ through belonging together, growing together, and serving together. These neighborhood groups are starfish communities that have a built-in vision for reproduction. The people in these groups are passionate to see others from their neighborhood join them and eventually become followers of Christ. Each time a cycle of the growth and reproduction flywheel is completed (see image below), a new neighborhood community group is born. As these groups spread over time, they reach additional neighborhoods, eventually reaching an entire city.

To begin cultivating a neighborhood environment, it helps to map out the neighborhoods in which your church members live. Oak Hills Church uses a program called Arena, which was designed by Christ's Church of the Valley in Peoria, Arizona.[7] It can be customized to your local area, and our team has outlined each of the unique neighborhoods of San Antonio—a total of 2,020 in all.

This program interfaces with our church member database program and allows us to drop "pins" in an appropriate neighborhood for each household in our database. Combining these visual maps of the neighborhoods of San Antonio with the locations of our church members allows us to see where our people are clustered geographically. It's a picture that paints a thousand words. When we see the pins clustering together, we begin to imagine what will happen when these "pins" of people come together. Our dream is that, just like in Acts 2, our church members will take on the responsibility of meeting needs within their neighborhoods, spreading the love of Jesus in practical and powerfully concentrated ways. If you don't have access to the latest technology, take a map of your city, attach it to a poster board in a prominent spot in your church, and ask your members to place their location pin on the map. In a few weeks, you will have a clear, visual map that shows the neighborhoods where your church is already present.

In addition to mapping locations, it's important to designate a champion to initiate and lead the formation of new neighborhood communities. While there is no single structure or method for doing this, neighborhood gatherings need a catalyst, a person who will model the vision and values of the group and possess the passion to see others experience them. This is the kind of person who wakes up each day with the formation of neighborhood communities as their driving goal, their number one work assignment. In smaller churches, this will likely be a committed volunteer. Larger churches like Oak Hills and Christ's Church of the Valley have multiple, full-time, designated neighborhood pastors who preside over regions of our city.

The specifics will vary depending on your context; what matters is that someone is set apart for the job — a person focused on the actual implementation and sustainability of the vision.

THE SIX-STEP PROCESS

How do you begin the transition from a centralized church structure to a hybrid structure, one that retains the strengths of both the campus and neighborhood contexts? At Oak Hills we are using the following simple, six-step process to help us in this transition. Other neighborhood-based community churches will undoubtedly have a somewhat different process, and that's OK. There truly is more than one way to do this! The key is to have a simple, accessible pathway that will help people engage your neighborhood vision in bite-size pieces.

Here are the six steps we encourage people to take.

Step 1: Be a good neighbor. It all begins with a commitment to the call: embracing the values and the way of life that will make your people good neighbors. This is a decision to take what God has given to you and is forming in you and offer it to other people for their sake. It's what we have talked about in this book — climbing out of the pool of individualism, isolation, and consumerism into a way of life that finds individual and satisfying purpose in aligning one's life to God's story.

If you — meaning anyone — embrace this challenge, you will need to start wearing a new set of glasses and learn to see your neighborhood with fresh eyes. You will need to start looking for opportunities to be considerate and helpful in the smallest of ways. You should be friendly, acknowledging people's presence with a wave and a smile as you enter and exit the neighborhood. You'll need to ask questions, seeking to learn about your neighbors by listening to their stories. You should make a decision, in advance, to say yes to as many invitations to dinners and birthday parties in the neighborhood as possible, much like Jesus did when he was invited to join the gatherings of his day. And as you walk the streets of your neighborhood, you should pray for the people in each house you pass. When you learn of a need, don't just say, "Keep warm and well fed."[8] Roll up your sleeves and look for tangible ways to help.

When a church commits to the royal commandment of Jesus — to love God and love neighbors — it should make the call clear for each member, providing tangible, practical suggestions for putting faith into action. Make sure no one is excluded or forgotten when you present the vision. Include suggestions for children, married couples, and singles. Think about what this looks like for those living in residential neighborhoods, as well as for those in apartments, condos, or assisted living. The more tangible and concrete the details you can provide, the better. You may even ask people to visit your website and register their decision to "love God and love neighbor" as a way of providing them with a weekly e-mail from your equipping team, giving practical advice and simple ideas, sharing the stories of others who are also doing this.

Step 2: Host a dessert. Your neighborhood pastors, whether staff or volunteers, should be proactively looking at your database and maps to see where there are pockets of households who live in the same neighborhood, apartment community, college dormitory, or condominium cluster. When at least three households are identified, the neighborhood pastor should find one of the households that would be willing to host a one-time dessert at their home. Invitations can be sent out to people in the neighborhood, along with a personal call to follow up on the formal invitation.

At the dessert, people can be asked to introduce their family members and to share which house they live in, how they came to the neighborhood, and how long they have lived there. The neighborhood pastor or community group leader takes a few minutes to share the vision of neighborhood community and some of the benefits, and then proposes the idea of forming a small group right in the neighborhood. The "ask" for those in attendance is to consider taking the next step and participating in a six-month experience that will provide an opportunity to see how all of this works, as well as an opportunity to get to know others better.

Step 3: Do a six-month trial. We have found the best way to handle this initial six-month experience is through the use of a DVD-based curriculum. Many people are willing to open their home as long as they don't have to go through the rigors of being trained to teach new material. Each of the six sessions (one session a month) lays out the vision for igniting the presence of Christ in the neighborhood, along with practical ideas and steps to take to fulfill this vision. Folks are given the opportunity to discuss what they have seen.

I've observed that it takes approximately seven get-togethers for people to begin to feel a connection. At first they are not sure about hanging with this new group of people or if they are willing to draw their community circle around their neighborhood. The dessert and the six-month curriculum give a person two simple steps to take before a long-term commitment is made. Providing these two low-commitment steps greatly increases the likelihood that a permanent group will be formed.

Step 4: Move ahead with *belonging together*. As the six-month experience is coming to an end, the neighborhood pastor or community group leader gets together with the small group to see if they want to keep on meeting. If the answer is yes, then three roles should be discussed:

1. **a point person:** the primary person the neighborhood pastor will connect with to offer help and assistance; ideally, this is the "connector" of the group
2. **an administrator:** the person primarily responsible for communication — getting out e-mails, evites, texts, or whatever form of communication works best for this group
3. **a host:** the person who makes sure a host home for each monthly gathering is available

When these roles are filled, the group is ready to transition into a more permanent monthly neighborhood gathering that follows the pattern laid out in chapter 11. As a reminder, here is what a monthly gathering could look like:

- **eat:** share a meal together
- **read the Word:** read and discuss a chapter in the Bible together
- **pray:** pray for each other's needs and the needs of people in your neighborhood
- **seek to serve:** ask, "What is God calling us to do to serve our neighbors and beyond?"

In addition to a monthly neighborhood gathering, each household is encouraged to have simple get-togethers with each other and to include other neighbors not involved in the gathering. This could be for a potluck dinner, a barbecue in the backyard, a Kentucky Derby party, a Super Bowl night, a board game night, or taking a simple walk in the evenings through the neighborhood for a little exercise. People should also be encouraged to engage in hobbies together, such as golfing, scrapbooking, playing tennis, or exercising. The ultimate experience is to plan a vacation together, such as a campout, a ski trip, a mission trip, a beach outing, or a foliage tour. The gathering is purposefully scheduled monthly so it provides the margin needed for these additional activities. These kinds of experiences are necessary for the health and success of the overall vision.

Step 5: Move ahead with *growing together*. Once a sense of connection and stability has developed in the group, the neighborhood pastor can seek to initiate opportunities for people to grow spiritually. The best way to accomplish this is by starting Bible studies. Most commonly, these are organized by gender. We have found that using DVD-based curriculum works great. The experience of watching the DVD offers the group an expert teacher on a topic without burdening any one person with the task of preparing a lesson.[9] Some curriculums, like the ones available for *The Story*, involve every member of the family.[10] But heed this word of caution: Not everyone involved in the monthly neighborhood gathering will be ready for, or have the margin for, a Bible study. That's OK. There is no need to pressure anyone. If the group is developing naturally, some will be interested in a Bible study, while others will be involved in other ways.

At the same time, let me offer a word of encouragement. Feel free to invite people in the neighborhood who aren't involved in your monthly gathering to attend the Bible study. You may be surprised to discover that many people really want to study the Bible; they just find church buildings too intimidating. You may also be surprised by the number of people in these Bible studies who eventually will want to join your monthly gatherings.

Step 6: Move ahead with *serving together*. A question is posed at each neighborhood gathering: "What is God calling us to do to serve our neighbors and beyond?" We have found that it often takes several months before anything tangible emerges. The neighborhood pastor can provide suggestions, but it is usually best to wait for a genuine need to emerge and a person from the gathering to lead the cause. The simplest idea is often to come alongside a neighbor in need and help them in practical, tangible ways.

Some ideas we have seen or been involved in include:

- arranging meals for a family in which the wife and mother just had major surgery
- organizing a 5K Fun Run in your neighborhood to raise money for a local organization
- taking care of the lawn and doing other projects for a widow in your neighborhood
- meeting with the principal of the local elementary school to see if there are any projects you could be involved in at the school
- volunteering together at a local organization that seeks to help the poor in your community
- pooling your resources to sponsor children in a particular village in the world through an organization like Compassion International or World Vision[11]

The ideas for serving people in your neighborhood are limitless. The power of each experience will be palpably felt as needs are met, Christ's love is shown in practical ways, and your group grows in depth of relationships. Eventually, you may even see new people come to faith in Christ and experience a revolution of the Belong-Serve-Grow flywheel as your group reproduces.

LINKING THE ENVIRONMENTS

As you develop your neighborhood context, it is important to find ways to link the two environments of campus life and neighborhood life. As you seek to link people involved and invested in the life of the campus, the centralized experience of the church, it's important to make sure the teaching that flows from the platform reinforces the mission. You will want to provide biblical and practical training that helps people catch the vision for living out their faith in their neighborhood. You may want to highlight stories of success that can be celebrated by the larger body of believers.

In addition, you can provide an undemanding pathway of involvement into neighborhood life. The easiest way to achieve this is to announce a simple reception after each service where people attending are assured they are welcome, will be helped in their spiritual journey, and are needed to fulfill the mission Christ has given the church. At this reception they can be invited to a discovery experience/class that walks them through the mission, vision, values, and strategy of the church and describes ways they can get involved in both the centralized campus life experience and the missional call to involvement in their neighborhood.

It's just as important, however, to link people who are involved in serving in their neighborhoods with the centralized ministry of a church. Keep in mind that this can be *any* local church, not necessarily your own church or campus. If a gathering established in a particular neighborhood is healthy and embraces a mind-set of outreach and inclusion, some people who attend other churches — and even some who do not attend church —

will enter into this community experience. Leaders of the neighborhood gatherings should make it clear to those attending that the goal is not to replace the weekly gatherings of God's people, nor is it in competition with the centralized ministry of the local church. At the same time, neighborhood gatherings do not exist to draw people back to a particular church; they exist to draw people closer to Christ. The monthly neighborhood gatherings are not recruitment arms of the centralized ministry, seeking to snatch away new church members to a building. They are simply an extension of the local church living out the presence and power of Jesus in the neighborhood.

Many people involved in your neighborhood gatherings will still want to attend regular services in a church building. There is nothing wrong with inviting people to visit your church. Keep in mind some practical matters when you make this invitation.

1. Give an invitation with no strings attached. This is for their benefit, not yours.
2. Offer to ride together if possible. If they're coming separately, tell them about the spaces available for visitors' parking and arrange a time and place to meet them.
3. Let them know ahead of time what they will experience at your church so they know what is coming. Remember, what seems normal to you may feel really strange to a newcomer who hasn't been to a church service in a long time.
4. If they have children who may want to try the children's ministry program, walk with them through the process. If you both have students in the home, encourage your students to host them and walk with them into the student service or class.
5. Sit together at the service.
6. Plan a time after the service to chat about their experience. Answer any questions they may have.
7. Invite them to come back. If they continue to enjoy the experience, encourage them to go through a discovery

class so they can fully understand and engage the mission of your church.

If a person or a family is not interested in attending any program in your church building, that's OK. Continue to partner with them on being Jesus to each other and to the rest of your neighborhood, and just trust the story that God is unfolding in their lives.

Our church has been careful to define our biblical mission in a broad statement that can be applied in many different ways: "We are the body of Christ, called to be Jesus in every neighborhood in our city and beyond." We witness to the person and work of Jesus in our neighborhoods in the hope that others will be touched by his presence. We theologically define the "presence of Christ" as a collection of believers, as small as two or three, who come together in Jesus' name to do his work.[12] We know that where his followers gather, God's Spirit is present and the work of Jesus is done. Our vision is both qualitative and quantitative. Quantitatively, we want the *presence* of Christ in every neighborhood in our city and a *decision* for Christ for every seeker. Qualitatively, we want the *maturity* of Christ in each disciple.

So get started! It's not hard to begin. Consider putting up a map of your surrounding area. Highlight the neighborhoods in which you are already involved and identify new locations where believers can work together to be the visible presence of Christ in that neighborhood. Ask the congregation to envision with you what it would be like to have every single neighborhood highlighted for the sake and cause of Christ. And pray for God to bring revival. God's plan to change this world is carried out by committed believers serving together to reach their neighborhoods in the power of the Holy Spirit.

Do you have a vision for your city to be transformed? Invite your people to share that vision.

Chapter 15
SUCCESSFUL MODELS

One of my greatest joys over the past ten years has been watching a number of leaders and congregations emerge with a strong vision for connecting and neighboring. The test of any new initiative is to see if others are able to adopt the core ideas and innovate where necessary to make them work in their own context of ministry. In this chapter, I'll highlight a few of the churches that have done just that—successfully made the vision presented in this book a reality in their own ministry context. These are the stories of *connecting* churches.

CHRIST'S CHURCH OF THE VALLEY, PEORIA, ARIZONA

Christ's Church of the Valley (CCV) was founded in 1982 by Don Wilson, a strong, competent leader and coach.[1] Under his leadership the church grew substantially in a suburb of Phoenix. Then in 2007, Wilson made a sudden and radical shift to neighborhood ministry. His conviction was that you should never catch up with your dream or you will return to your past. He and his team read the first edition of *The Connecting Church*, as well as *Making Room for Life* and a host of other resources. They caught the vision and eventually brought this ministry approach to the neighborhoods in their city.

They have used a basic, simple structure to implement this vision. Similar to what was presented in the previous chapter, they focus on only two environments—the campus environment (they have three) and the neighborhood environment. The campus facilities are first-class, and they host dynamic worship services and children's and student ministries, as well as a ministry called life training classes—special classes and support groups strategically training and equipping members.

They also focus on the neighborhood. They define a neighborhood group as a "gathering with people we live by and share life with, in order to reach our unsaved neighbors for Christ."[2] Their neighborhood groups are distinct from the campus ministries, but they are all characterized by the central three elements of the Acts 4 community flywheel.

1. They *belong* together and do life together as a small group of believers living in proximity to one another. These groups meet weekly.
2. They *grow* together, primarily by having a group discussion on the sermon from the weekend.
3. They *serve* together by simply being intentional about meeting the needs of their neighbors and the needs of their community around them.

Christ's Church of the Valley has nine full-time neighborhood pastors on staff and a robust and committed volunteer team in place to help them pursue this vision. To date, they have an average of eighteen thousand people attending their two campuses each weekend and over ten thousand people involved in six hundred neighborhood groups sprinkled throughout their community!

What CCV has accomplished through God's provision and blessing is nothing short of a miracle. They have developed a thriving neighborhood ministry in an existing megachurch. In their training material, they declare "neighborhood ministry will move believers from being consumers to contributors"—directly attacking the prevailing consumerism of our culture. Even more surprising, the church has not declined in attendance. In 2011, CCV was the tenth largest church in America and the fifth fastest-growing church in America. In 2011, they grew by 4,049 people, more than any other church in the United States.[3]

Though my experience suggests it takes somewhere between five to seven years to make the shift from a centralized focus to a hybrid model that embraces the connecting church vision, CCV has done it in three years. Granted, the first two years were filled with turbulent waters, but they have stayed the course, never taking their eyes off the final destination. In the past two years, they have truly turned the corner. I attribute this to God's grace, as well as to Don's commitment as the founding senior pastor to a vision that combines neighborhood ministry with evangelistic fervor. The first time I had lunch with Don and his wife, Sue, I saw a sparkle in their eyes as they talked about their own relationship with a next-door neighbor. This personal modeling by those in church leadership communicates far more about the connecting church vision than a thousand sermons can.

Recently, I ran into a former member of CCV at one of our Oak Hills campuses. He and his wife had relocated to our area and had connected with our campus in the small town of Fredericksburg, Texas. I immediately noted that the vision for neighborhood ministry had captured this couple, even though they no longer attended CCV. Not only were they now involved in a neighborhood group; they were the hosts. They planned on using their new home in Texas the same way they had in Arizona. Their vision and passion for community life, first implanted at CCV, were now bearing fruit in our church.

I believe Christ's Church of the Valley is one of the best expressions of the connecting church vision, and I'm not ashamed to brag about how God has worked through their faithfulness. When I started this journey more than twenty years ago, I had no other church leaders on my radar to go to for help. Now, when we want to train our teams here at Oak Hills, we send them to CCV to learn from their great and courageous work.

TRI-LAKES CHAPEL, MONUMENT, COLORADO

If you find the eighteen-thousand-member size of Christ's Church of the Valley a bit overwhelming, and you aren't sure your church experience could match what they're doing, take a look at the wonderful expression of the connecting church vision among the faithful folks at Tri-Lakes Chapel in Monument, Colorado.[4] Tri-Lakes Chapel is still a fairly large church for its area. In fact, it is the largest congregation in the mountain community of Monument, just north of Colorado Springs. The town's population was 4,903 in 2009, and the church runs about one thousand people in their weekend services. That's an impressive percentage of penetration into a community!

What is the vision of Tri-Lakes Chapel? "Biblical community on every street in the Tri-Lakes area." Three years into implementing their vision, they have thirty-five neighborhood gatherings they refer to as base camps. Approximately 60 to 65 percent of the congregation's members are engaged in some form of community ministry in their local neighborhoods. What's even more impressive is the rate at which they are growing. When I talked to Tom Anthony, the executive pastor and chief architect of their community vision, he told me they were launching eight new base camps *that month alone.*

A base camp community exists to help participants build intimacy with God, experience a sense of family with each other, and cultivate the ability to reach out intentionally to neighbors. The format of the weekly, intergenerational base camp meeting is simple. For the first hour they share a meal. During the second hour they read the Scriptures or spend the hour praying for needs in the group or neighborhood. Sometimes they just chill out with a game night. The planned meeting is simply an excuse to be together and experience life together. Each week, through teaching and stories, they are called to make room for life and for each other, to enter into each other's space in the neighborhood. They are invited and encouraged to take walks together, play out in the front yard, smell the roses, and enjoy unplanned conversations with their neighbors.

They have successfully weathered the storms of change and are now seeing numerical growth, but more important, they are seeing real life change in their people. They will be the first to acknowledge it hasn't been easy. Not everyone in the church really wants to love their neighbors. But when people make the decision to obey and do what Jesus is asking them to do, lives are changed and transformed.

During my visit, I heard a story of a young, outgoing couple in one of the neighborhoods who came to know Christ, which completely changed the direction of their lives. When they hear stories like this, the Tri-Lakes leaders tell me they have no regrets about the decision to take their church to the streets. I believe Tri-Lakes Chapel is on target to see amazing kingdom fruit in the Monument and Colorado Springs area as they stay the course.

THE DENVER CITY MOVEMENT

About fifty miles north of Tri-Lakes Chapel is another group of pioneers led by Dave Runyon, a group that has pursued a vision for something larger than neighborhood community life. Dave and his friends have set out to change an entire city.[5] Several years ago, a group of church leaders got together with a shared vision to make a difference in their city — the Denver metro area. At one of their early get-togethers, they asked the mayor of Arvada, a northern Denver suburb, to meet with them. They asked the mayor two questions: "What is your dream for this city?" and "What is one thing we can do to help?" They didn't anticipate his answer. The mayor gave them this challenge: "Figure out a way where we can just become better neighbors."

The pastors turned to each other in surprise. Had the mayor just challenged them to do the very thing they wanted to do, the very thing Jesus had challenged them to do — to love their neighbors? Building off that conversation, they started a neighboring *movement,* bringing together churches in the Denver metro area and teaching practical, intentional ways for people to be better neighbors. The first step they share is quite simple: get to know the names of the eight neighbors who live right around you!

Today, this neighboring movement (they call it "Building Blocks") in the Denver area has grown to forty churches, and they've launched two significant initiatives. The first is a citywide, three-week sermon series on the topic of neighboring. Each year, the forty partner churches commit to doing the same three-week series that focuses on loving your neighbor. It is a series that puts "shoe leather" to Jesus' big idea. The vision is cast, and highly practical action steps are given. Having so many churches on the same page for three weeks in the same city talking about the love of Jesus is potent indeed!

The second major initiative is the creation of a unique online map that identifies all the neighborhoods in the Denver metro area. Those who wish to participate in the movement can declare their intention to love their neighbors — officially "raising their hand" — by placing a digital pushpin that identifies their home on the map. They get to see who has also registered their intention from the other thirty-nine churches. The goal is for participants to reach out and connect with the folks near them and join forces to get to know and love their neighbors.

Here is a letter from a family that raised its hand to the call:

> In our neighborhood we have two families at Faith, one at Spirit of Christ and one from Grace. It certainly has been a blessing to discuss the neighboring ideas that we are talking about in this shared sermon series!
>
> As a group, we started thinking about hosting a gathering for our neighbor, and we decided to do an outdoor movie night. My wife, Gina, used some old fabric to sew together a screen that covered our entire garage. One of our other neighbors supplied a DVD player, projector, and a sound system, and we invited others over to take in a movie. It ended up having a sort of "drive-in" feel.

The four families are hoping to put together a schedule for our neighborhood this summer and expand the movie nights to include some grilling and eating before the movie. We are excited to see where things go from here.

For others looking for ideas, I would simply pass on this "drive-in" idea. It really isn't that hard to pull off, and it's a lot of fun. When we've done it in the past, we get a lot of participation from many neighbors as everyone brings a lawn chair and comes out to enjoy a nice night.

Andrew

Though the movement began as a top-down strategy of senior leaders in churches across the city, it has morphed into a grassroots initiative that continues to build momentum. Word of this citywide movement has spread all the way to Duluth, Minnesota, where churches have replicated and refined the model.[6]

CHURCH @ THE SPRINGS, HOUSTON, TEXAS

Brad Gartman is a courageous pioneer and one of my heroes.[7] We worked together in Fort Worth, Texas, as I was beginning to formulate the connecting church vision in the 1990s. Brad was one of our area pastors, and he oversaw the creation of community groups and home groups in the North Fort Worth area. He did a fantastic job. Brad's vision was to start a church with a lifelong friend in the Houston area, so he left us with our blessing. Later, he paid me a visit and asked how I would go about planting a church based on the connecting church concept.

Though I had never attempted such a thing, I had a few ideas about how it might be done, which I shared with Brad. I told him I would start by forming neighborhood groups, establishing the neighborhood environment in the church, and then, after those were firmly established, I would transition the church into a centralized worship service. To my delight and surprise, Brad and his friends took the idea and ran with it. To be honest, I was quite jealous of what they were doing and longed to be involved in some way.

Brad and his co-pastor each started a neighborhood gathering in their respective neighborhoods. As time went on, they started a few more neighborhood groups. In addition to serving each other and the needs that arose in their neighborhood, they collectively volunteered at the local YMCA. When it came time to start a centralized worship service for the five neighborhood groups, the Y let them use their space for free!

At The Springs, there is an almost rhythmic challenge they give to all who wish to be involved:

- **daily:** Brad and his team challenge families to gather around the table for a meal each day to connect and share. This makes a strong statement that the family is the first of all small groups.
- **weekly:** There is a weekly gathering of believers in each neighborhood where they share a meal together, a word of hope, and a challenge to reach out.
- **twice a month:** Every other week there is a corporate gathering for neighborhood groups for worship, instruction, and sharing stories.
- **monthly:** There is a monthly call to chill out with your neighbors. It's all about relationships, not programs.

While Brad and his team have had many trying seasons on their journey, I believe what they have implemented is the future of the church. As more and more leaders choose this path, we will do well to seek to learn from the ones brave enough to go before us.

■ ■

Yes, without question, one of the greatest joys I've experienced over the past ten years is seeing how people have reshaped and implemented the ideas from the first edition of *The Connect-*

ing Church. People have taken those ideas and have transformed existing churches and planted new churches with a strong focus on connecting together in community. Seeing the ways God has used this book and the ideas in it has been humbling, but it is also a source of great joy to know that God is still at work forming and shaping the future of his people. I never imagined that God would take these ideas and use them to change his church. I am grateful to God for the opportunity to participate in what he is doing. May the tribe of radical followers of Christ, those who take to heart Jesus' command to love their neighbors, increase and flourish!

That said, there is still much for us to learn. We've learned some things over the years, enough so that when I close my eyes I can see where the path will lead, even though we aren't quite there yet. In the next chapter, I'll give you some hints about the future and where I think God is taking us next.

Chapter 16

IMPLEMENTING THE STARFISH MODEL

Several chapters ago, I mentioned how the book *The Starfish and the Spider* gave me a picture for a hybrid model of church that combined the best of this vision with our existing, centralized model of ministry here in the United States. That book opens with the fascinating story of how Spain, under the leadership of Hernán Cortés in 1519, overtook the organized and centrally controlled Mexican empire of the Aztecs led by Montezuma and later the Incas led by Atahualpa. What took centuries to build was destroyed in just two years.[1]

Yet when the Spanish conquistadors moved north to repeat their command performance against another group of natives, they ran into a "different animal" altogether — the Apaches. Unlike the centrally organized Aztec tribes, the Apache nation was not centrally organized. They lacked a single commander like Montezuma. They couldn't be defeated simply by taking their gold and killing a single leader. The Apache tribes existed in a decentralized structure held together across wide geographic regions by common values and cultural norms modeled by a spiritual leader they called a Nant'an. But the Nant'an was not irreplaceable. Whenever the Spanish would kill one of them, a new one would emerge from the tribe and take the mantle of leadership.

From 1680 to 1914, first the Spanish, then the Mexicans, and finally the Americans were unable to defeat the Apache tribes.

Then something changed in 1914. As Brafman and Beckstrom write, "Here's what broke Apache society: the Americans gave the Nant'ans cattle. It was simple. Once the Nant'ans had possession of a scarce resource—cows—their power shifted from symbolic to material. Where previously the Nant'ans had led by example, now they could reward and punish tribe members by giving and withholding this resource."[2] In other words, the cow changed everything. Once the Nant'ans gained authoritative power, they began fighting each other for seats on newly created tribal councils and started behaving more and more like would-be "presidents of the Internet." Again, Brafman and Beckstrom observe, "Tribe members began lobbying the Nant'ans for more resources and became upset if the allocations didn't work out in their favor. The power structure, once flat, became hierarchical, with power concentrated at the top. This broke down Apache society."[3]

The church today displays a similar story line. Jesus began his church with a decentralized structure. Though there were leaders, they were each commissioned with the same task: reaching the world by preaching the gospel and starting small communities of Jesus followers in the cities they visited. As you read the book of Acts, you see little gatherings of believers around Jerusalem who are being taught by spiritual leaders called apostles. The gatherings continued to grow, as day after day the Christians gathered in the public square of the temple courts and went house to house, teaching the dynamic new principles of Christianity.[4] Luke gives this report: "So the word of God spread. The number of disciples in Jerusalem increased rapidly, and a large number of priests became obedient to the faith."[5]

When severe persecution broke out against the church in Jerusalem, the movement wasn't destroyed by the death of its members. Instead, it spread outward and multiplied to new locations like Judea and Samaria. Luke writes, "Those who had been scattered preached the word wherever they went."[6] Luke continues to emphasize this theme throughout the book of Acts:

"But the word of God continued to spread and flourish."[7]

"The word of the Lord spread through the whole region."[8]
"So the churches were strengthened in the faith and grew daily in numbers."[9]

Even as the apostle John was receiving his final revelation around AD 90 (the final book of the Bible, God's revealed Word), the church was continuing to grow. The story doesn't end with the early church. Historian and sociologist Rodney Stark has taken a long and deep look at how the obscure, marginal Jesus movement became the dominant religious force in the Western world in just a few centuries. He concludes that Christianity grew at a rate of 40 percent per decade. By his calculations, "There would have been 7,530 Christians in the year 100, followed by 217,795 Christians in the year 300 and 6,299,832 Christians by the year 300."[10] This number represents 10.5 percent of the total population. By AD 350, Christianity reached 56.5 percent of the world's estimated 60 million people.[11]

Fast-forward several hundred years from the apostle John's day to AD 327, and we see the starfish structure of the early church movement begin to morph into an institutionalized spider organization. In other words, this is the year the church received her cow, like the Nant'ans of the Apaches.[12] Constantine, the emperor of Rome, converted to Christianity and began commissioning the construction of church *buildings*. His motives were undoubtedly pure and God-honoring. Frank Viola states, "He did so to promote the popularity and acceptance of Christianity. If the Christians had their own sacred buildings — as did the Jews and the pagans — their faith would be regarded as legitimate."[13]

Sadly, since the days of Constantine, the growth of the church has largely been tied to the buildings it inhabits. Through our attachment to physical buildings, we have developed centralized hierarchies and now carry with us much of the baggage that comes with them. May I be so bold as to suggest that disempowering the church as a decentralized movement has been the strategy of our enemy? Over the years, while buildings have played many positive roles and have packed more people in them than a house could ever hold, this single shift changed the church from an open, easily reproducible movement to a closed, centralized organization. Fast-forward to today with the rise of fragmented living, and the church building has now become largely isolated and irrelevant from the everyday life of our culture.

I believe our dependency on buildings and centralized structures is one of the primary reasons the individual American church has found it difficult to rise above a 25,000-member ceiling while Christian churches around the world are able to reach and exceed this number, numbering as high as 250,000 members. But this is only possible with a decentralized structure that is not dependent on physical structure.

It's no surprise to anyone that the church in America is in decline. The first wave of decline has hit the mainline denominational churches and the Catholic Church. Now a second wave of decline is hitting the ranks of the evangelical church as well.[14] Loss in numbers means loss in cash, and for centralized churches with staff and buildings to support, this is a cause for concern.

In addition to the visible decline in church attendance, we are seeing the inclining influence of "nonphysical" forms of communication with the Internet. Brafman and Beckstrom suggest that "decentralization has been lying dormant for thousands of years. But the advent of the Internet has unleashed this force ... [and] serves as an open platform on the back of which a wide variety of starfish organizations can be launched."[15] This is especially true of the church because of its decentralized roots.

John Wesley, founder of the Methodist Church, captured in the 1700s the idea of a network of communities connected together. Arguably, Wesley led the first multisite congregation. He delivered his messages in person, and for fifty years he traveled forty-five hundred miles a year, mostly on horseback, teaching an average of twice a day.[16] Today, we can instantly and simultaneously transfer information, teaching, audio, and video in HD quality in an interactive format to almost anywhere in the world at a relatively small cost. I wonder what Wesley would have been able to accomplish with his vision for reaching the masses via decentralized communities if he had been able to employ the technology available today—computers, flat-screen televisions, Roku, Apple TV, and mobile devices. I believe his head would have been spinning with possibilities and his heart would have been pounding for kingdom advancements. And so should ours.

THE STARFISH CHURCH

Though we've looked at the value in hybrid models of church that combine centralized structures and buildings with decentralized neighborhood communities, I believe that in the long term, this hybrid model is a transitional model for ministry. Over the long haul, the future of the church is in a return to smaller, decentralized communities that carry within them the whole concept of the church. Like a starfish, they are attached to other communities, but can easily reproduce if cut off or separated from the others. Each starfish church carries in it the values, vision, and creedal commitments of historical Christianity, and it carries on the mission of the church empowered by the Holy Spirit.

The basic strategy that drives these decentralized communities is the Acts 2 structure we have been considering, without the presence of a central building:

Belong

In these decentralized gatherings, a group of believers from two or more households (ideally in the same neighborhood) comes together for "fellowship and the breaking of bread." They intentionally commit to representing and igniting the loving presence of Christ in their neighborhood, city, and world. Weekly, they gather around a shared meal. Optimally, everyone gathers around the same table, family style. If this isn't possible, then everyone gathers in a circle prior to the meal to offer thanks. This meal is centered on Christ and the remembrance of his death. At the beginning of the meal, the breadbasket is passed and everyone takes a slice or roll. Then the host offers a simple prayer of thanks for the bread, which represents the body of Christ.[17] Everyone takes a bite of the bread in honor of Christ. The food is served up, and the conversation, laughter, and chaos of a festive meal begin.

Three simple questions are always asked during the meal:

1. How are you doing spiritually?
2. How can we pray for you and our neighbors?
3. How is God calling us to serve each other, our neighbors, our city, and the world?

The meal comes to a close with a time of prayer. One or more people pray for the requests and celebrations that were shared. The host then takes his cup and finishes the prayer time by remembering the blood of Christ that was shed on the cross for the forgiveness of sins. Everyone takes one final drink in honor of Christ.[18]

Grow

I recommend *not* adopting the sermon model of communication as you pursue the vision of a self-sustaining neighborhood community. As Frank Viola and George Barna have argued from their research, the sermon as we know it today was not part of the first-century church. It was likely adopted from pagan cultures sometime in the third century.[19] Unlike the celebration of the Lord's Supper, it is not an essential element of the gathering.

This does not mean there should be no teaching. It is clear that the early church was devoted to the teaching of the apostles through reading and discussing the apostles' letters and reading stories from the four gospel accounts. This is what I recommend. In fact, at each of our neighborhood gatherings we read a chapter from a New Testament letter and then discuss how this chapter is resocializing us as a community toward God's ultimate vision.

As soon as your adults commit to listening to a sermon, you create a need for a separate children's ministry. In addition, the sermon style of communication may not be the most effective way of communicating the truth people need to know for living out the Christian life. One of the key struggles I've had over my twenty-plus years as a pastor of large churches meeting in buildings is how to teach a sermon series that speaks to the spiritual development needs of vastly diverse audiences.

There is one final struggle with the sermon as a mode of communication. Most people don't attend church weekly. My colleagues in ministry typically measure commitment as attendance at church worship services *twice* a month. Often, new people are entering into a message in the middle of a series. Even if our teaching has a developmental sequence to it, people don't always grasp the nuances of development in a single message, much less over a series of messages. The outcome? Despite winsome and engaging preaching, most people are still not getting it. Our churches are filled with biblically and spiritually illiterate congregations.

I believe there is a better way.

Years ago, Rozanne and I were seriously thinking about homeschooling our two youngest sons but were terrified we would ruin them. When we looked at the classrooms, the budgets, the buildings, and the staffing of our public, private, and Christian schools, it seemed ludicrous to think the two of us could come close to providing what our children needed educationally.

About that time, George Barna was scheduled to be in town to conduct a seminar. He traveled with his wife, Nancy, and their two daughters, who were homeschooled. We offered to host them in our home, and, naturally, we probed them on the subject. Nancy said something that got our attention. She said we were not comparing apples to apples. Building-based schooling is a totally different paradigm of education from homeschooling. First, these schools must deal with "herding" because of the numbers. Imagine the average class with twenty-five students. When you strip away the time it takes to check in, have lunch, take recess, answer questions, go to the bathroom, and get to the next class, there is a relatively small amount of time for instruction and learning.

Second, these schools use a grading system. Kids miss school, but the teacher moves forward. The child does the makeup work, and all seems to be well. But even though at the end of the semester one child gets an A, another a B, another a C, and another a D, they all pass and all move to the next grade—even if they haven't mastered the lessons to be learned. By the time students graduate from high school, many have met the minimum requirements and may even have earned decent grades, but they don't have a solid educational foundation to build on.

But homeschooling is different. There is no herding. There is an enormous amount of efficiency. And homeschooling is built on mastery of a subject, not on achieving passing grades. Each child works at his or her own pace. When they have functionally mastered a section for a topic, they move forward. Many students in building-based education, however, are moving forward on a rocky foundation. Is it any wonder that the percentage of National Merit Scholars among homeschoolers is strikingly higher than among building-based students? One in twenty-five graduates of a homeschool program is a National Merit semifinalist. The national norm is one in two hundred for public school graduates.[20]

The next day, Nancy Barna turned over the reins to Rozanne and me to teach her daughters. There is nothing like actual experience to make a point. We both survived the experience, and, in fact, over the next year we homeschooled our two younger sons. To our amazement, they completed their school activities, including homework, by 1:00 p.m. most days and were able to complete two years of math in a single year!

Why do I mention this? Because I believe the same opportunity exists for churches willing to make the radical shift to a new way of doing church. Our churches don't have to be filled with biblically and spiritually illiterate congregations. And it all starts by identifying what Christians need for a solid biblical and spiritual foundation. I see four resources and experiences as essential:

1. *The Story* **curriculum for adults, teens, and children.** This chronological journey through the Bible enables the learner to capture the one story of God, communicate it to others, and identify how they fit into God's story.[21]

2. *The Story: Going Deeper.* The goal of this innovative study Bible experience is to teach learners how to access the Bible for themselves. Six QR code video sessions give instruction on where the Bible came from, how it is organized, and how to use tools to read and study it. Participants are invited to engage in 180 chronological readings through the Bible to hone their newfound skill and to break in their Bibles like well-worn pairs of Texas boots.[22]

3. **Think.Act.Be — 30 Core Characteristics.** This is a journey through the thirty biggest ideas of the Bible that lead a person to be more like Jesus, which is the ultimate mission in life for the individual and the community. Collectively, these thirty items make up the common creed of the community. Ten of the ideas deal with our beliefs (think like Jesus); ten address our practices (act like Jesus); and the final ten deal with virtues (be like Jesus). See the appendix for more details. Each idea is anchored in a creedal statement that creates a common language within the community. It takes roughly four sessions to work through each idea. The goal is functional competency in the idea, i.e., the disciple grasps the idea and is able to put the driving principles into practice in daily life.

4. **A Personal Growth Plan.** Once learners have a base of biblical and spiritual knowledge, the goal is to spend the rest of their days getting these principles operational and functional in their daily lives. It is one thing to get into the Bible; it is another thing to get the Bible into you! *The Christian Life Profile Assessment Tool* is designed to help people evaluate their lives and develop intentional spiritual growth plans.[23] Once areas have been targeted for growth, the plans lead the disciples to a host of best-practice resources to aid them on their journey.

It is significant that each of these four foundational experiences is designed for the entire family—not only enabling every member of the family to be developed, but putting parents back into the driver's seat and giving them responsibility for discipling their children. These experiences eliminate the need for highly complicated children's ministries that are dependent on church buildings to succeed.

When a new member joins a starfish church, they begin working at their own pace, starting with an introduction to the story line of the Bible. When they come to the weekly gathering, they report on where they are in the journey and how they are doing and ask for help if needed. The community is there to encourage and to help them.

Children raised in this kind of intentional spiritual community will mature into adulthood:

- knowing God's story, knowing how to tell that story, and understanding how they fit into God's story
- equipped to access and study the Bible for themselves
- with a solid understanding of the thirty big ideas in the Bible that form us into Christlikeness
- committed to pursuing an ongoing personal spiritual growth plan for their lives

Serve

As these little bands of believers belong and grow in a neighborhood, they will eventually begin to serve. As in the hybrid model, they look to serve each other, their surrounding neighbors and community, and even the world. But there are two main differences from the hybrid model: (1) this community does not use any of its margin in time to attend or serve the ministry programs of a centralized building, and (2) the community has 90 percent of its financial resources available to fund their calling to meet needs.

In most churches, 90 percent of the offerings are used to fund the building, debt, salaries, and internal programming of the church. A mere 10 percent is distributed to causes external to the church—ministry to the poor and international, cross-cultural evangelistic ministry. Some well-managed churches are able to free up 20 percent of their budget to be distributed to these types of efforts, and a few radical churches make it their practice to give away 50 percent. In all of these cases, the decision about where to invest these resources is centralized: "You give; we spend."

In a decentralized structure, everyone is encouraged to give 10 percent of their overall offering to support the network that provides teaching and resources to them. This leaves 90 percent of their resources to distribute as God leads them as a community. The group can and should seek to use the resources to:

- meet each other's needs as they arise
- purchase resources for spiritual and biblical growth
- meet the needs of neighbors as they arise
- fund organizations, projects, and people in the local community
- support a chosen international mission endeavor
- fund a short-term mission trip for the entire group to the area you are supporting

Discerning needs, giving, and taking ownership for distributing money is an important part of the call to outreach and the discipleship process. Church groups that engage in this process will grow both individually and together as a body.

The goal in stewarding resources is not just to exercise financial wisdom; it's to get people personally involved in making these decisions. As the group decides what God is calling them to engage in, they should always look for ways to involve their children in the process. The experience of a child who grows up in a community where it is normative for them, their parents, and the larger community to serve others is extraordinarily valuable. Children should see and experience service to the surrounding community, the poor, and even the world. This will go a long way toward discipling them in becoming like Jesus and preparing them to carry the torch as they become adults.

As this community begins to turn the flywheel, eventually there will be people around them who want to become a part of their gathering. Some will already be Christ followers; others will be seekers, taken aback by the groups' "love for one another," who want to know if they can also follow Jesus and become a part of this spiritual family.[24] With inclusivity as a driving value of this community, the answer is always yes. When this happens, a revolution occurs.

THE STARFISH NETWORK

Imagine, for a second, what it would look like to have one thousand of these starfish-structured churches scattered across the United States. If the average gathering (with children) is approximately thirty people networked together in a way similar to our current multisite church structure, this church would be the second-largest church in the United States.[25] A church of this size will collect about $30 million in offerings. But unlike the traditional church budget plan, with buildings to pay for and staffing to fund, most of the money given ($27 million) will be distributed to meet the needs of people instead of covering building mortgages and program budgets.

A network like this exists to connect and resource each local neighborhood gathering. It lacks a hierarchical structure with top-down authority over these gatherings. Instead, the local gatherings are started by believers who decide to join the network because they agree with their common mission, vision, values, and creed. The network seeks primarily to support the churches in two tangible ways, all covered by the limited financial support provided by the churches.

Technology

While this is an ever-moving target, again, it is possible today to deliver good, high-quality teaching content directly into the home through a Roku device or Apple TV. The use of such technology allows a small church community to create a channel and download just about any kind of programming they wish—sermons, training, stories, updates, programming, and movies. The box or strip can be moved to any location with Wi-Fi service. Programs can be shown directly on a television or computer screen in HD quality. One of the network's primary tasks is to create, place, and maintain the resources that teach and equip members in ways that the local gathering is unable to do.

Pastor

With the voluntary monthly support of the local gatherings, the network provides a pastor who serves a particular geographic area. These pastors help to start, guide, and minister to a local network of neighborhood churches. They assist through training, resourcing, encouraging, and problem solving. In many ways, this pattern of teaching is similar to the model of the visiting apostle or evangelist of the first-century house church, much like the work that Timothy and Titus did in Ephesus and Corinth during the first century.

What I've shared above is only a thumbnail sketch of the possibilities I see for the launch of a fresh expression of the church in America, yet one with ancient roots. While I am living out some of this vision in my neighborhood, we at Oak Hills are still connected to about eight different church buildings in our community. In the future, this outline for a starfish model is where I see some of our church heading. In the meantime, we can celebrate the both/and approach of the hybrid model. As more and more churches adopt the hybrid model of ministry, we will begin to see a new generation of Christians rise up—Christians who have been trained and equipped to live out their faith, not in a centralized model of Christianity dependent on top-down leadership and physical buildings, but in one that is rooted in the core beliefs and practices of the early church. I am convinced this new way of doing church will lead to the emergence of starfish-structured networks.

In other words, I have hope that the best days of the church are yet to come.

AFTERWORD

I was rummaging through some files a few years back and found a paper I had written during my last year in seminary. The assignment was to construct a vision statement and plan for my life. The year was 1986. Rozanne and I had been married for five years, and our only child at the time — our daughter, Jennifer — was two years old. To the best of my ability and with lots of prayer, I crafted a vision for my character development, marriage, children, work, personal life, church, parents, time, and money. But that isn't all. As I paged through this old paper, I found my first written vision for neighborhood life. Here is what I wrote:

- Develop good, wholesome relationships with my neighbors; have spontaneity as a goal; go against the grain of culture.
- Decorate our home with country warmth.
- Leave as much time as I can to visit neighbors and to do small favors for them; expect them to drop over unexpectedly.
- Try to influence them toward a personal relationship with Jesus Christ; emphasize relational lifestyle evangelism.

As I read those words written in 1986, I was struck again at just how countercultural all of this was at the time and how it continues to be a radical vision for community. I was also reminded that it wasn't an idea in a seminary classroom. It wasn't something I had read about in a book. And it certainly wasn't my idea first.

A new family had moved into my neighborhood, two doors down from where we were living at the time. This family was nonchurched. Jesus and the church were not on their short list of priorities and concerns. Yet as we got to know our new neighbors, we formed an organic, life-giving relationship with them. Our lives overlapped naturally as we spent time together in the neighborhood. For months, I pondered how to invite this family to come to church and then to be a part of our church-sponsored small group, but I could never quite navigate that transaction. It felt awkward at best.

It was during this early season that I wrote the above vision statement. I remember how one day it dawned on Rozanne and me that instead of taking our neighbors to the church, we could try bringing the church to our neighbors. It was this insight that ignited a personal revival in our lives. Each step we took in this direction convinced us it was the right journey for us to be on as a family. In 1994, I cautiously brought this same idea to Pantego Bible Church, and for the next eleven years we engaged in a trial-and-error dance to make the transition. Eventually, we were successful.

Then in 2001, I received the privilege of sharing my journey in the first edition of *The Connecting Church*. In 2005, my wife and I wrote a companion book titled *Making Room for Life*. Without putting much thought into it, I found myself quickly becoming that "neighborhood guy." There was Mr. Rogers for kids, and then there was Rev. Frazee for the church.

Then in 2005, we accepted an invitation to bring these concepts to Willow Creek Community Church in the Chicago area. While ministering there, I received one of the most complimentary e-mails I've ever received from a member of Pantego Bible Church. I still have it today.

> Randy,
>
> I know you're getting tons of e-mail right now, but I wanted to join the well-wishers and tell you how excited I am about your new opportunity at Willow Creek. I have always thought that your special gift and purpose is to communicate and implement the idea of place-based community, especially in metro areas where it seems to be most needed.
>
> I also wanted to tell you something that I hope will encour-

age you, though it may not sound very encouraging right off, so keep reading! Here it goes: It doesn't really matter to me that you're leaving, and I don't know that your departure will make a big difference in my life. (Keep reading!) You're a nice guy to listen to on Sunday morning, but you're not in my "circle," and I barely know you. I would be upset by the departure of the Hammetts, Chambers, McLeans, or Seibolds (all in my home group or community group) since those guys are such a significant part of my life and spiritual development, but I'll be fine without you! They're the reason I get out of bed on Sunday morning! I say all these things quite bluntly just to confirm and emphasize that your vision has been fully implemented here at Pantego and you can move on, knowing that it will continue to thrive and bring glory to God as people share in one another's lives and invest those lives in the kingdom of God.

Go in grace and buy a good coat!

Terrie Moore

Unfortunately, our journey in Chicago was cut short and was ultimately unsuccessful. As I mentioned earlier, I find it takes at least five to seven years to implement this shift in a church. Willow Creek, with its large size and deeply rooted organizational structures, is not your average church. During our time there, however, we saw the launch of several pockets of dynamic community throughout neighborhoods in the northwest suburbs of Chicago. More important, we know lives were forever changed by the courage of the folks who dared to take their faith to the streets. Our time in Chicago reminded me that God's call is not for us to be successful; it's for us to be faithful with what he gives us. We need to trust that he will take care of the rest. Growth is never our work. It is the Lord who adds to our number daily those who are being saved.[26]

Now, as of the writing of this book, we have found ourselves back in Texas for the past four years. We have been living in San Antonio, working with Oak Hills Church as they begin their own journey into the neighborhoods of San Antonio. I believe we are making amazing progress, but it will be another two to three years before we hit our full stride.

Yet, as I've said, during these past ten years I've had great joy as I've watched other churches pick up on the ideas found in my writings and take them in new directions. The extraordinary success of places like Christ's Church of the Valley in Peoria, Arizona, reminds me that God calls some to plant the seed, some to water, and some to harvest, but God is behind each step in the process.[27] Just today I had a conversation with a young minister who is following the leading of his heart and is exiting the centralized (spider) church with all of its security to take up a new missional adventure with a neighborhood church. As he shared his young family's radical decision, he was breathing heavily, not just with fear, but with excitement. He knows he is simply being obedient to the undeniable urging of his soul. For a brief moment I squinted at him and saw a reflection of myself as a young man.

As this second edition of *The Connecting Church* is releasing, it is 2013. Twenty-seven years have passed since I naively wrote down my first vision for neighborhood living. I am now in my fifties, and we have raised four children and are empty nesters.

Do I have any regrets?

Not a single one. My greatest satisfaction is to look at the outcome of this vision as we have lived it out in our family and passed it along to our four children. This vision has been good for them and for our family. They are all walking with God, and we are very much connected as a family. I am confident that what we've planted in them will continue to develop and be nurtured in their lives.

In 1986, our daughter was two years old. In 2013, she turns twenty-nine. When she was two, she didn't have much to say about our decision to connect in our neighborhood. At twenty-nine, she does. Read her words:

> Growing up, I was often asked, "What is it like being a pastor's daughter?" I was always confused at how to answer that

question because I never knew what it was like not to be one. I assumed that we were just as normal as the next family.

As I got older, I began to realize that growing up in my family was very different from most families in one specific way. We knew our neighbors and hung out with them on a daily basis. I never remember dinners with just the six of us family members. We usually had at least one neighbor at our dinner table. There were the occasional rare nights when we did not have someone joining us for dinner, but shortly after dinner we were all outside in our front yard listening to my dad play the banjo. Neighbors would be out walking and come over to sing and talk with us. I don't remember many nights spent without fellowshipping with the people who lived close to me. This holds true for all four of the neighborhoods I have lived in with my parents.

I found out even more so just how unique this "knowing your neighbors" thing was when I went off to college. When I would tell my friends stories about back home, they would tell me, "Oh, it must be so nice living so close to extended family." My response was, "No, these are my neighbors who are like our aunts and uncles." First, I got the puzzled look! Then came the request to go home with me on a weekend to experience it for themselves. Needless to say, after the first time I brought a friend home, I never went home from college without someone joining me. I began to understand that the majority of people did not live this way. How awesome it was that my parents have so much to do with all of it! I was given such a wonderful gift of having a family that lives outside of themselves.

Now, looking back at how I grew up, I am extremely aware as to how knowing the people around me has affected my life in such a positive way. I always had someone close by that I trusted if I ever needed anything. I witnessed how our community would surround and love on a family when they were going through a hard time. It was as if our whole neighborhood was going through it with them. There was never a time I remember that I felt alone with no one to reach out to. I know a completely different definition of family than most people in this world.

I now am married and have a beautiful daughter, who is two. From the minute she was born, I knew she would be so blessed to never know anything other than community. Shortly after her birth, I began a job with a nonprofit organization that promotes people gathering in their apartment communities for events centered on the idea of community and knowing your neighbors. We felt so drawn to the ministry and all that it is doing to connect one of the world's most disconnected societies. Because of my experiences growing up, I have developed a passion to help people see the importance of community—not only help them see it but show them how easy it is to live it. I cannot imagine life any other way.

So to sum it up, I will never have an answer for what it is like to be a pastor's child, but I can answer the question "What was it like growing up in a neighborhood where everyone knows who you are and what you are about?" The answer: It is life changing and probably one of the most fulfilling, satisfying things you can have in your life. It has brought the utmost joy to my life, and I can already see the wonderful effect it is having on my daughter! We are blessed beyond words! I truly feel sorry for those who don't give something like this a shot. I mean, what do you have to lose? Trust me, you have more to gain from the people who live next door than you could ever imagine.

If you are a mom or a dad, you must know how fulfilling these words are for me to read. This is what a living legacy is all about—one that I'm proud of and grateful to God for giving me.

But don't count me out just yet. There is some tread left on my tires, and I plan to continue to "put the pedal to the metal" in the next phase of the connecting church vision in my life with Rozanne. I don't know exactly where it is going to take me—I never have—but I am staying on this path to the end until God calls me to take up residence in my final and eternal neighborhood in the new kingdom. And if we never get to live in the same neighborhood on this earth, I look forward to getting to know you better in the neighborhood to come.

ACKNOWLEDGMENTS

Writing a book on community is certainly not a solo endeavor. I have many people to thank for making this work a reality—both the first edition and now the second.

First and foremost, I thank Jesus Christ. I have never recovered from your gracious offer of life to me in 1974.

Second, I dedicate this book in memory of my mother, Ruth Ann Frazee, who died in December 1999. Her simple faith in God has spoken to the depths of my soul. My father, Ralph; brother, Don; two sisters, Teresa and JoAnn; and I miss her so much. She sacrificed her whole life for us so we could succeed. In this small way, I want to publicly acknowledge my gratefulness for her life.

I thank my wife, Rozanne. I never dreamed when I met her at the age of fifteen that one person could so perfectly and courageously love a guy like me. Words cannot describe how deeply I feel about my bride of more than thirty years, but I will spend the rest of my life trying. Rozanne also edited the manuscript of both editions before the editors at Zondervan got hold of it. Her efforts have saved me a great deal of time and embarrassment, and once again she has made me look good.

Our four children—Jennifer, David, Stephen, and Austin—truly inspire and motivate me. It was my vision for our life together that caused me to pursue these principles of community so passionately—not only to write about it but, more important, to live it.

Ten years later, our family is growing. I am delighted and thankful to God for bringing Desmond and Gretchen to our family table. God has weaved his perfect will and brought two of our four children wonderful soul mates. Then there is our first grandchild—

Ava! Grandparenting is way underrated; I truly didn't see this coming. I would have had this book out six months earlier if I hadn't dropped my pen every time she came into my home office. I can't help myself. Instead of writing about connection, I opted to do a bit of connecting with this little human being who brings me so much joy. When the 3.0 version of this book comes out ten years from now, I am anticipating a quiver full of grandkids. No pressure, kids!

We have lived in four neighborhoods since this vision overtook our lives in 1986: Waggoner Drive, Bay Club, the Village of Barrington, and Village Green. The people God intentionally put into our lives in each of these wonderful spaces have not only become our closest friends; their belief and participation in the vision have personally motivated me to stay the course. Without these people, we would have given up a long time ago. These are the true heroes of the connecting church movement.

I've had the great fortune of having more people than I deserve come alongside and support me unconditionally. You held me when I was tired and discouraged, overlooked my quirks, and gave me more than one break. You saw more of God's vision in me than I could see myself. Thank you, Bob Buford, Mike and Bev Reilly, the late George Gallup Jr., Dallas Willard, Scott and Donita Jones, Rick and Lyn Veigel, Larry Ivey, Ryall and Jane Tune, Gary and Linda Lawrence, and Pat and Rita Ballow. To those I have forgotten, once again I give you an opportunity to overlook my imperfections.

I thank my assistant, Nancy Brister, who has been with me since 2005, for managing the tedious edits on the manuscript. For instance, endnotes suck the life right out of me, so in addition to typing and editing, Nancy drains her battery managing endnotes for my benefit. I am deeply grateful she made the move with my family from Chicago to San Antonio. For her kindness, I prayed that God would bring her a loving husband. He did in the gracious form of Eddie. I like to think this has made up for all the long hours and hardship I have caused her. Eddie, thanks for loving Nancy and her two beautiful daughters and for your helpful edits on the manuscript.

I could not have implemented these ideas in real life without the aid of the staffs I've worked alongside in the three churches I have served over the last twenty-plus years. In most cases I introduced them to the vision; they embraced it, modeled it, and led others to experience it through the gifts God has given them. I thank my God every time I think of you.

Then there is Max Lucado. Your invitation to come to San Antonio to partner with you has been one of the greatest blessings of my life. It is my privilege to let the folks who read your many books know you really are that gracious, authentic, and humble in real life. The spiritual collision of our lives has been super-life-giving to me. The deep friendship Rozanne and I are developing with you and Denalyn is proof positive that God loves and cares about my personal life.

What has been a true encouragement is all the people who read the first edition of this book and embraced it and did something about it in their own lives and leadership: Don Wilson of Christ's Church of the Valley in Arizona, Tom Anthony of Tri-Lakes Chapel in Colorado, Brad Gartman of Church @ The Springs in Houston, and Jon Peacock of Mission Church in Chicago, to name but a few. These men and women have taken the best of what I have to offer, added their own insights, and in many ways taken the connecting church to a whole new level. Nothing can be more humbling and satisfying. May our tribe increase!

Finally, I want to thank Zondervan for your continued belief in me and this vision. It all began with my editor, Jack Kuhatschek, a dozen years ago at a dinner in Fort Worth. I bought you one of the best steaks that Texas cattle can offer, Jack. You not only saw the book but the vision. I am grateful that God has "expanded your territory." To my friend John Raymond, who runs point on all things "Randy"; Ryan Pazdur, my new editor; Dirk Buursma; and the rest of the team at Zondervan, I thank you for giving me the opportunity over this last decade to share what God has passionately put on my mind and heart.

Randy Frazee,
San Antonio, Texas

Appendix

THINK.ACT.BE —
30 CORE CHARACTERISTICS*

THINK LIKE JESUS (BELIEFS)

Trinity

Creed: I believe the God of the Bible is the only true God —
Father, Son, and Holy Spirit.

> *"May the grace of the Lord Jesus Christ, and the love of
> God, and the fellowship of the Holy Spirit be with you all."*
> 2 Corinthians 13:14

Salvation by Grace

Creed: I believe a person comes into a right relationship with God
by his grace, through faith in Jesus Christ.

> *"For it is by grace you have been saved, through faith — and
> this not from yourselves, it is the gift of God — not by works,
> so that no one can boast."* Ephesians 2:8 – 9

Authority of the Bible

Creed: I believe the Bible is the Word of God and has the right to
command my belief and action.

---

*Based on *The Christian Life Profile Assessment Tool* (Grand Rapids: Zondervan, 2005).

"All Scripture is God-breathed and is useful for teaching, rebuking, correcting and training in righteousness, so that the servant of God may be thoroughly equipped for every good work." 2 Timothy 3:16–17

Personal God

Creed: I believe God is involved in and cares about my daily life.

"I lift up my eyes to the mountains—where does my help come from? My help comes from the LORD, the Maker of heaven and earth." Psalm 121:1–2

Identity in Christ

Creed: I believe I am significant because of my position as a child of God.

"Yet to all who did receive him, to those who believed in his name, he gave the right to become children of God." John 1:12

Church

Creed: I believe the church is God's primary way to accomplish his purposes on earth today.

"Instead, speaking the truth in love, we will grow to become in every respect the mature body of him who is the head, that is, Christ. From him the whole body, joined and held together by every supporting ligament, grows and builds itself up in love, as each part does its work." Ephesians 4:15–16

Humanity

Creed: I believe all people are loved by God and need Jesus Christ as their Savior.

"For God so loved the world that he gave his one and only

Son, that whoever believes in him shall not perish but have eternal life." John 3:16

Compassion

Creed: I believe God calls all Christians to show compassion to those in need.

"Defend the weak and the fatherless; uphold the cause of the poor and the oppressed. Rescue the weak and the needy; deliver them from the hand of the wicked." Psalm 82:3–4

Eternity

Creed: I believe there is a heaven and a hell and that Jesus Christ is returning to judge the earth and to establish his eternal kingdom.

"Do not let your hearts be troubled. You believe in God; believe also in me. My Father's house has many rooms; if that were not so, would I have told you that I am going there to prepare a place for you? And if I go and prepare a place for you, I will come back and take you to be with me that you also may be where I am. You know the way to the place where I am going." John 14:1–4

Stewardship

Creed: I believe everything I am or own belongs to God.

"Command those who are rich in this present world not to be arrogant nor to put their hope in wealth, which is so uncertain, but to put their hope in God, who richly provides us with everything for our enjoyment. Command them to do good, to be rich in good deeds, and to be generous and willing to share. In this way they will lay up treasure for themselves as a firm foundation for the coming age, so that they may take hold of the life that is truly life." 1 Timothy 6:17–19

ACT LIKE JESUS (PRACTICES)

Worship

Creed: I worship God for who he is and what he has done for me.

> *"Come, let us sing for joy to the LORD; let us shout aloud to the Rock of our salvation. Let us come before him with thanksgiving and extol him with music and song. For the LORD is the great God, the great King above all gods. In his hand are the depths of the earth, and the mountain peaks belong to him. The sea is his, for he made it, and his hands formed the dry land. Come, let us bow down in worship, let us kneel before the LORD our Maker; for he is our God and we are the people of his pasture, the flock under his care."*
> Psalm 95:1–7

Prayer

Creed: I pray to God to know him, to lay my request before him, and to find direction for my daily life.

> *"Come and hear, all you who fear God; let me tell you what he has done for me. I cried out to him with my mouth; his praise was on my tongue. If I had cherished sin in my heart, the Lord would not have listened; but God has surely listened and has heard my prayer. Praise be to God, who has not rejected my prayer or withheld his love from me!"*
> Psalm 66:16–20

Bible Study

Creed: I study the Bible to know God, the truth, and to find direction for my daily life.

> *"For the word of God is alive and active. Sharper than any double-edged sword, it penetrates even to dividing soul and spirit, joints and marrow; it judges the thoughts and attitudes of the heart."* Hebrews 4:12

Single-Mindedness

Creed: I focus on God and his priorities for my life.

"But seek first his kingdom and his righteousness, and all these things will be given to you as well." Matthew 6:33

Biblical Community

Creed: I fellowship with other Christians to accomplish God's purposes in my life, others' lives, and in the world.

"All the believers were together and had everything in common. They sold property and possessions to give to anyone who had need. Every day they continued to meet together in the temple courts. They broke bread in their homes and ate together with glad and sincere hearts, praising God and enjoying the favor of all the people. And the Lord added to their number daily those who were being saved." Acts 2:44–47

Spiritual Gifts

Creed: I know and use my spiritual gifts to accomplish God's purposes.

"For just as each of us has one body with many members, and these members do not all have the same function, so in Christ we, though many, form one body, and each member belongs to all the others. We have different gifts, according to the grace given to each of us. If your gift is prophesying, then prophesy in accordance with your faith." Romans 12:4–6

Giving Away My Time

Creed: I give away my time to fulfill God's purposes.

"And whatever you do, whether in word or deed, do it all in the name of the Lord Jesus, giving thanks to God the Father through him." Colossians 3:17

Giving Away My Money

Creed: I give away my money to fulfill God's purposes.

> *"But since you excel in everything — in faith, in speech, in knowledge, in complete earnestness and in the love we have kindled in you — see that you also excel in this grace of giving."* 2 Corinthians 8:7

Giving Away My Faith

Creed: I give away my faith to fulfill God's purposes.

> *"Pray also for me, that whenever I speak, words may be given me so that I will fearlessly make known the mystery of the gospel, for which I am an ambassador in chains. Pray that I may declare it fearlessly, as I should."* Ephesians 6:19 – 20

Giving Away My Life

Creed: I give away my life to fulfill God's purposes.

> *"Therefore, I urge you, brothers and sisters, in view of God's mercy, to offer your bodies as a living sacrifice, holy and pleasing to God — this is your true and proper worship."* Romans 12:1

BE LIKE JESUS (VIRTUES)

Love

Creed: I unconditionally and sacrificially love and forgive others.

> *"This is love: not that we loved God, but that he loved us and sent his Son as an atoning sacrifice for our sins. Dear friends, since God so loved us, we also ought to love one another. No one has ever seen God; but if we love another, God lives in us and his love is made complete in us."* 1 John 4:10 – 12

Joy

Creed: I have inner contentment and purpose in spite of my circumstances.

"I have told you this so that your joy may be in you and that your joy may be complete." John 15:11

Peace

Creed: I am free from anxiety because things are right between God, others, and me.

"Do not be anxious about anything, but in every situation, by prayer and petition, with thanksgiving, present your requests to God. And the peace of God, which transcends all understanding, will guard your hearts and your minds in Christ Jesus." Philippians 4:6–7

Patience

Creed: I take a long time to overheat and endure patiently under the unavoidable pressures of life.

"Whoever is patient has great understanding, but one who is quick-tempered displays folly." Proverbs 14:29

Kindness/Goodness

Creed: I choose to do the right things in my relationships with others.

"Make sure that nobody pays back wrong for wrong, but always strive to do what is good for each other and for everyone else." 1 Thessalonians 5:15

Faithfulness

Creed: I have established a good name with God and with others based on my long-term loyalty to those relationships.

"Let love and faithfulness never leave you; bind them around your neck, write them on the tablet of your heart. Then you

will win favor and a good name in the sight of God and man." Proverbs 3:3–4

Gentleness

Creed: I am thoughtful, considerate, and calm in dealing with others.

> *"Let your gentleness be evident to all. The Lord is near."*
> Philippians 4:5

Self-Control

Creed: I have the power, through Christ, to control myself.

> *"For the grace of God has appeared that offers salvation to all people. It teaches us to say 'No' to ungodliness and worldly passions, and to live self-controlled, upright and godly lives in this present age, while we wait for the blessed hope — the appearing of the glory of our great God and Savior, Jesus Christ."* Titus 2:11–13

Hope

Creed: I can cope with the hardships of life and with death because of the hope I have in Jesus Christ.

> *"We have this hope as an anchor for the soul, firm and secure. It enters the inner sanctuary behind the curtain, where our forerunner, Jesus, has entered on our behalf."*
> Hebrews 6:19–20

Humility

Creed: I choose to esteem others above myself.

> *"Do nothing out of selfish ambition or vain conceit. Rather, in humility value others above yourselves, not looking to your own interests but each of you to the interests of the others."*
> Philippians 2:3–4

NOTES

Preface to the Second Edition

1. See "Timeline of Computer History," Computer History Museum, www.computerhistory.org/timeline/?category=cmptr; "Laptop," Wikipedia, http://en.wikipedia.org/wiki/ Laptop#History; "Personal Computer," The Great Idea Finder, www.ideafinder.com/history/inventions/compersonal.htm (accessed September 5, 2012).

Chapter 1: The Loneliest Nation on Earth

1. George Gallup Jr., *The People's Religion* (New York: Macmillan, 1989), 253.

Chapter 2: Created for Community

1. Commission on Children at Risk, *Hardwired to Connect: The New Scientific Case for Authoritative Communities* (New York: Institute for American Values, 2003), 16.
2. Ibid.
3. Ibid.
4. Ibid., 17.
5. Helen Colton, *The Gift of Touch* (New York: Putnam, 1983), 33.
6. *Hardwired to Connect*, 20.
7. Ibid., 19.
8. Ibid., 21.
9. George Gallup Jr., *Emerging Trends* 19.3 (March 1997).
10. Hebrews 10:25, emphasis added.
11. Matthew 16:18.
12. Wayne A. Meeks, *The First Urban Christians: The Social World of the Apostle Paul* (New Haven, Conn.: Yale Univ. Press, 1984), 78.

13. From a speech given by Lyle Schaller at a Leadership Network Conference in Ontario, California, October 1998.

Chapter 3: The Problem of Individualism

1. Transcribed from *Antz*, directed by Eric Darnell and Tim Johnson; screenplay by Todd Alcott, Chris Weitz, and Paul Weitz (Universal City, Calif.: DreamWorks, 1998).
2. See Philippians 3:7–11.
3. See Philippians 2:3–4.
4. Cited in John L. Locke, *The De-Voicing of Society: Why We Don't Talk to Each Other Anymore* (New York: Simon & Schuster, 1998), 125.
5. See E. D. Hirsch Jr., *Cultural Literacy* (Boston: Houghton Mifflin, 1987).
6. Locke, *De-Voicing of Society*, 122. The time immediately following World War II represented a prosperous era for the American economy. The resources paid for the advancement of the superhighway system, which, under Dwight Eisenhower's presidency, made mobility possible and diminished rooted relationships. This boom time also sparked the rise of suburban living, where close-knit neighborhoods were forfeited in favor of individual privacy. In addition, technological developments, such as central air and heating, refrigeration, and the television, have prompted many suburbanites to stay cocooned in their homes for the few hours they are actually there each day. The reality of easy mobility has resulted in Americans spending much of their time in the automobile and not in the home. I'll have more to say about this in part 2.
7. Peter Block, *Community: The Structure of Belonging* (San Francisco, Berrett-Koehler Publishers, 2008), 5.
8. See Hirsch, *Cultural Literacy*, xvii.
9. See Genesis 2:18.
10. Locke, *De-Voicing of Society*, 202–3.
11. See Robert Wuthnow, *Sharing the Journey: Support Groups and America's New Quest for Community* (New York: Free Press, 1994).
12. 2 Peter 1:3–11.
13. George Barna, "The Barna Update" (July 12, 2000), biweekly e-mail report.

14. Dallas Willard, *The Spirit of the Disciplines* (New York: HarperCollins, 1988), 16.
15. John 1:17.
16. See John 4:1–42.
17. See John 8:1–11.
18. See Ephesians 4:15.
19. Ephesians 4:16.

Chapter 4: Characteristics of a Common Purpose

1. Wayne A. Meeks, *The First Urban Christians: The Social World of the Apostle Paul* (New Haven, Conn.: Yale Univ. Press, 1983), 75.
2. Meeks, *First Urban Christians*, 76.
3. Commission on Children at Risk, *Hardwired to Connect: The New Scientific Case for Authoritative Communities* (New York: Institute for American Values, 2003), 9–10.
4. Ibid., 6.
5. Ibid., 35.
6. Meeks, *First Urban Christians*, 93. An argot is a private vocabulary used within a community as a way to summarize entire paragraphs of meaning by means of a single word or collection of words.
7. Deuteronomy 6:20–25.
8. See 1 Corinthians 11:26.
9. *Hardwired to Connect*, 14.
10. Acts 2:44.
11. Acts 2:42.
12. Acts 4:32.
13. Ephesians 4:4–6.
14. Lyle Schaller, "Every Part Is an 'I': How Will the Body Function in an Age of Rising Individualism?" *Leadership Journal* (Fall 1999), 29.
15. Quoted in Colin Dye, "The Roots of Spiritual Decline," *Direction* 127 (April 2012): 30.
16. C. S. Lewis, *Mere Christianity* (New York: Macmillan, 1943), 163, 169–70, emphasis added.
17. Galatians 4:19; see Ephesians 4:15–16; Colossians 1:28–29.
18. Dallas Willard, *The Spirit of the Disciplines* (New York: HarperCollins, 1988), 16.
19. See Romans 12:1–2; Philippians 4:8.

20. See Philippians 4:9; 1 Timothy 4:8; Hebrews 5:13–14.
21. See Philippians 2:5.
22. See Galatians 5:22–23.
23. Philippians 2:1–5.
24. See 2 Peter 1:3–11.
25. Willard, *Spirit of the Disciplines*, 16.

Chapter 5: Rediscovering Biblical Purpose

1. Dallas Willard, *The Spirit of the Disciplines* (New York: HarperCollins, 1988), 16.
2. See Stanley Grenz, *The Social God and the Relational Self: A Trinitarian Theology of the* Imago Dei (Louisville: Westminster John Knox, 2001).
3. See 1 John 4:8.
4. Galatians 5:22–23.
5. Genesis 1:26–27, emphasis added.
6. Genesis 1:31.
7. Genesis 2:24.
8. Matthew 3:17.
9. See Matthew 26:28.
10. See Romans 5:12–19.
11. See Revelation 21–22.
12. See Deuteronomy 6:4–9.
13. See Romans 12:5; 1 Corinthians 12:12, 27; Ephesians 3:6; 4:12, 15; 5:23; Colossians 1:24; 3:15.
14. See John 17; Ephesians 4:4.
15. See Galatians 5:19–21.
16. Ephesians 5:29–32.
17. Matthew 18:20.
18. See Matthew 28:19–20.
19. See Vincent Branick, *The House Church in the Writings of Paul* (Wilmington, Del.: Glazier, 1989), 42.
20. Acts 2:42–47.
21. See Robert Banks, *Paul's Idea of Community*, rev. ed. (Peabody, Mass.: Hendrickson, 1994), 81.
22. See Ephesians 4:15–16.
23. See Rodney Stark, *The Rise of Christianity* (New York: HarperCollins, 1995), 7.

24. See Grenz, *Social God*, 11.
25. 1 Corinthians 12:12–20, 27.
26. John 3:30.
27. See Revelation 21–22.
28. See Titus 1:5–9.
29. Robert D. Putnam and David E. Campbell, *American Grace: How Religion Divides and Unites Us* (New York: Simon & Schuster, 2010), 141–42.
30. George Gallup Jr., *Emerging Trends*, 19.2 (February 1997): 1.
31. Pew Forum on Religion and Public Life, "U.S. Religious Knowledge Survey," September 28, 2010, http://pewresearch. org/pubs/1745/religious-knowledge-in-america-survey-atheists-agnostic (accessed September 5, 2012).
32. See David Kinnaman, *You Lost Me* (Grand Rapids: Baker, 2011), 22.

Chapter 6: The Problem of Isolation

1. Sally Jacobs, "Years after Neighbors Last Saw Her, Worcester Woman Found Dead in Home," *Boston Globe*, October 27, 1993, emphasis added.
2. Liz Stevens, "Suburbia: Are Suburbs Hazardous to Your Health?" *Fort Worth Star-Telegram*, March 8, 1997, 6.
3. Quoted in ibid., 6.
4. Ibid.
5. Philip Langdon, *A Better Place to Live: Reshaping the American Suburb* (New York: HarperCollins, 1994), 1.
6. James Howard Kunstler, "Home from Nowhere," *The Atlantic Monthly* (September 1996), 43.
7. John L. Locke, *The De-Voicing of Society: Why We Don't Talk to Each Other Anymore* (New York: Simon & Schuster, 1998), 118–22.
8. Ibid., 122.

Chapter 7: Characteristics of a Common Place

1. Transcribed from *Jurassic Park*, directed by Steven Spielberg; screenplay by Michael Crichton and David Koepp (Universal City, Calif.: Universal City Studios and Amblin Entertainment, 1993).
2. Jeremiah 6:16, emphasis added.

3. John L. Locke, *The De-Voicing of Society: Why We Don't Talk to Each Other Anymore* (New York: Simon & Schuster, 1998), 122.

4. See Luke 10:25–37.

5. Quoted in Edward J. Blakely and Mary Gail Snyder, *Fortress America: Gated Communities in the United States* (Washington, D.C.: Brookings Institution Press, 1997), 35.

6. Acts 2:42.

7. Locke, *De-Voicing of Society*, 132.

8. Jim Petersen, "What Is a Church?" *Discipleship Journal* 12.3 (May/June 1992): 92.

9. Jeffrey Weiss, "Your Church Is Largely What It eats, Author Says," *Dallas Morning News*, July 24, 1999, Religion section.

10. Acts 2:46.

11. Eberhard Arnold, *Why We Live in Community* (Farmington, Pa.: Plough, 1995), 17.

12. See William J. Doherty, "Overscheduled Kids, Underconnected Families: The Research Evidence," www.puttingfamilyfirst.org/research.php (accessed October 10, 2012). This study shows that during the period of 1981 to 1997, participation in children's structured sports doubled from two hours, twenty minutes per week to five hours, seventeen minutes per week. During this same time period, family mealtime declined from nine hours a week to eight hours per week. The study reports a 33 percent decrease over three decades in family mealtimes.

13. See Henri Nouwen, *The Inner Voice of Love: A Journey through Anguish to Freedom* (New York: Doubleday, 1996), xiii–xiv.

14. Larry Crabb, *Connecting: A Radical New Vision* (Nashville: Word, 1997), 23–24.

15. Jenell Williams Paris, "Why I No Longer Live in a Community," *re:generation quarterly* 5.2 (Summer 1999): 10.

Chapter 8: Rediscovering Neighborhood

1. Francis Bacon, *Bacon's Essays* (New York: Macmillan, 1889), 62.

2. See Genesis 3:8.

3. Zechariah 8:4–5.

4. See John 1:14.

5. John 1:14 MSG.

6. See Isaiah 7:14.

7. See Luke 24:1–3.
8. See Luke 24:37–39.
9. See 1 Corinthians 15:3–8.
10. Revelation 21:1–3.
11. See Philippians 3:20–21.
12. Robert Wuthnow, *Sharing the Journey: Support Groups and America's New Quest for Community* (New York: Free Press, 1994), 276.
13. Ibid., 276–77.
14. See "Kangaroo Care," Wikipedia, http://en.wikipedia.org/wiki/Kangaroo_care (accessed September 5, 2012).
15. Tim Jarvis, "How Happiness Is Contagious," *O, The Oprah Magazine* (May 2009), www.oprah.com/spirit/Happiness-is-Contagious (accessed September 5, 2012).
16. See Ping Ren, "Lifetime Mobility in the United States: 2010," (November 2011), www.census.gov/prod/2011pubs/acsbr10-07.pdf (accessed October 10, 2012).
17. See Acts 2:47.
18. Matthew 7:12.
19. Wayne A. Meeks, *The First Urban Christians: The Social World of the Apostle Paul* (New Haven, Conn.: Yale Univ. Press, 1984), 105.
20. Lyle Schaller, *Discontinuity and Hope: A Radical Change and the Path to the Future* (Nashville: Abingdon, 1999), 11.

Chapter 9: The Problem of Consumerism

1. Matthew 7:12.
2. See Matthew 6:24.
3. John L. Locke, *The De-Voicing of Society: Why We Don't Talk to Each Other Anymore* (New York: Simon & Schuster, 1998), 156.
4. Quoted in ibid., 156.
5. See Matthew 5:39–41.
6. 1 Corinthians 6:1–8.
7. Locke, *De-Voicing of Society*, 154.
8. See Exodus 20:17; Colossians 3:5.
9. Exodus 20:17.
10. Philip Langdon, *A Better Place to Live: Reshaping the American Suburb* (New York: HarperCollins, 1994), 240.
11. See Philippians 4:13.

Chapter 10: Characteristics of Common Possessions

1. Acts 4:32–37.
2. Acts 5:1–2.
3. Acts 4:32.
4. See Psalm 24:1; Colossians 1:16; 1 Timothy 6:17–19.
5. Quoted by Martin Marty in *Context* (a biweekly newsletter he produced from 1969 to 2010).
6. Matthew 4:4.
7. See John 6:35.
8. 2 Corinthians 8:13–15.
9. See 1 Samuel 15:22.
10. Psalm 37:4.
11. Luke 12:48.
12. Quoted in John L. Locke, *The De-Voicing of Society: Why We Don't Talk to Each Other Anymore* (New York: Simon & Schuster, 1998), 137.
13. See Titus 2:1–15.
14. See "Suicide and Older Adults," Illinois Department of Public Health (March 2011), www.idph.state.il.us/about/chronic/Suicide-Older_Adults.pdf (accessed September 5, 2012).
15. Dieter and Valerie Zander, "The Evolution of Gen X Ministry," *re:generation quarterly* 5.3 (Fall 1999): 17.
16. Philippians 2:1–5.
17. 1 John 3:16–20.
18. Eberhard Arnold, *Why We Live in Community* (Farmington, Pa.: Plough, 1995), 18.
19. Matthew 16:24–25.
20. See Edward J. Blakely and Mary Gail Snyder, *Fortress America: Gated Communities in the United States* (Washington, D.C.: Brookings Institution Press, 1997), 31.
21. Arnold, *Why We Live in Community*, 13.

Chapter 11: Rediscovering Authentic Community

1. Matthew 6:33.
2. Acts 17:26–27 NCV.
3. See Ephesians 5:32.
4. See "The Importance of Family Dinners VI," The National Center on Addiction and Substance Abuse at Columbia

University (September 2010), www.casacolumbia.org/upload/201 0/20100922familydinners6.pdf (accessed September 5, 2012).

5. Acts 2:47.

Chapter 12: Mistakes I've made ... Lessons I've Learned

1. Peter F. Drucker, *The Daily Drucker* (New York: HarperCollins, 2004), 343.
2. Ibid., 341.
3. Randy Frazee, *Making Room for Life* (Grand Rapids: Zondervan, 2003).
4. Rozanne and Randy Frazee, *Real Simplicity* (Grand Rapids: Zondervan, 2011).
5. Malcolm Gladwell, *The Tipping Point: How Little Things Can Make a Big Difference* (New York: Back Bay, 2002), 38.
6. Ibid., 41.
7. See 1 Corinthians 16:19; see also Acts 18:26; 2 Timothy 4:19.
8. Gladwell, *Tipping Point*, 53.
9. Cited in Ori Brafman and Rod A. Beckstrom, *The Starfish and the Spider: The Unstoppable Power of Leaderless Organizations* (New York: Penguin, 2006), 121.
10. Jay Walljasper, *The Great Neighborhood Book: A Do It Yourself Guide to Placemaking* (Gabriola, British Columbia: New Society, 2007), 142.
11. Quoted in ibid., 142.
12. Ibid, 6.
13. Quoted in Peter Block, *Community: The Structure of Belonging* (San Francisco, Berrett-Koehler, 2008), 26.

Chapter 13: Choosing a Path

1. Ori Brafman and Rod A. Beckstrom, *The Starfish and the Spider: The Unstoppable Power of Leaderless Organizations* (New York: Penguin, 2006).
2. 2 Samuel 7:5–7.
3. See Matthew 27:51.
4. See 1 Corinthians 6:19.
5. See Matthew 18:20.
6. See Acts 2:14–41.

7. *The Story: The Bible as One Continuing Story of God and His People* (Grand Rapids: Zondervan, 2011), www.thestory.com.

8. National Night Out promotes police and community partnerships for safer neighborhoods; for more information, visit www.natw.org/nno/.

9. Francis Schaeffer, *The Mark of the Christian* (Downers Grove, Ill.: InterVarsity, 1970), 17.

Chapter 14: Implementing a Hybrid Vision

1. Paraphrased from "Affirmation of the Vocation of the Baptized in the World," in *Welcome to Christ: Lutheran Rites for the Catechumenate* (Minneapolis: Augsburg, 1997), 60.

2. Learn more at www.thestory.com.

3. I worked with Zondervan to develop a study Bible to accomplish this objective. Check out *The Story: Going Deeper* at www.zondervan.com.

4. To accomplish this critical need, I developed the *Christian Life Profile Assessment Tool* (published by Zondervan), which contains a section on developing a personal plan for spiritual growth.

5. See Larry Crabb, *Connecting: Healing for Ourselves and Our Relationships* (Nashville: Word, 1997), xvi.

6. See Acts 2:47.

7. Visit Christ's Church of the Valley's website at www.ccvonline.com.

8. James 2:16.

9. For access to great DVD-based Bible and topical studies, check out www.bluefishtv.com.

10. Check out *The Story* products and resource library at www.thestory.com.

11. Learn more at www.compassion.com and www.worldvision.org.

12. See Matthew 18:20.

Chapter 15: Successful Models

1. Check out www.ccvonline.com.

2. Quoted in the training packet of Christ's Church of the Valley, Peoria, Arizona, www.ccvonline.com.

3. "The 100 Largest Churches in America," *Outreach* (2011 edition), 35.

4. Tri-Lakes Chapel, Monument, Colorado, www.trilakeschapel.org.

5. See Jay Pathak and Dave Runyon, *The Art of Neighboring* (Grand Rapids: Baker, 2012); visit www.artofneighboring.com.
6. Visit www.artofneighboring.com and select City Maps in the top right-hand corner to see the work in Duluth.
7. Check out Church @ the Springs, http://churchatthesprings. wordpress.com/.

Chapter 16: Implementing the Starfish Model

1. See Ori Brafman and Rod A. Beckstrom, *The Starfish and the Spider: The Unstoppable Power of Leaderless Organizations* (New York: Penguin, 2006), 16–17.
2. Ibid., 121.
3. Ibid., 151–52.
4. See Acts 5:42.
5. Acts 6:7.
6. Acts 8:4.
7. Acts 12:24.
8. Acts 13:49.
9. Acts 16:5.
10. Rodney Stark, *The Rise of Christianity* (New York: HarperCollins, 1995), 6.
11. Ibid., 7.
12. See Robin Lane Fox, *Pagans and Christians* (New York: Knopf, 1987), 667–68.
13. Frank Viola and George Barna, *Pagan Christianity? Exploring the Roots of Our Church Practices* (Wheaton, Ill.: Tyndale House, 2008), 18.
14. See Robert D. Putnam and David E. Campbell, *American Grace: How Religion Divides and Unites Us* (New York: Simon & Schuster, 2010), 141–42, 147.
15. Brafman and Beckstrom, *Starfish and the Spider*, 6–7, 98.
16. Tom Hermiz Evangelistic Association, "John Wesley: Itinerant Evangelist," www.tomhermiz.com/john-wesley:-itinerant-evangelist (accessed September 5, 2012).
17. See 1 Corinthians 11:23–24.
18. See 1 Corinthians 11:25.
19. See Viola and Barna, *Pagan Christianity?* 91.

20. Cited in "College and Beyond," HomeSchoolInfo.org, www.homeschoolinfo.org/collegeandbeyond.htm (accessed September 5, 2012).
21. Check out *The Story* products and resource library at www.thestory.com.
22. Check out the details at www.zondervan.com by searching for *The Story: Going Deeper.*
23. Visit www.zondervan.com and search for *The Christian Life Profile Assessment Tool.*
24. See John 13:35.
25. "The 100 Largest Churches in America," *Outreach* (2011 edition), 35. Lakewood Church is listed as the largest church in the United States with 43,500 in attendance. North Point Community is listed second with 27,429 in attendance.
26. See Acts 2:47.
27. See 1 Corinthians 3:6.